f

3 0132 01016883 4

This book is due for return on or before the last date shown below.

D1470801

Who is in Charge Here?

Further Misadventures of an RAF Officer

EDWARD CARTNER

Woodfield Publishing

First edition, published in 2002 by

WOODFIELD PUBLISHING
Woodfield House, Babsham Lane, Bognor Regis
West Sussex PO21 5EL, England.

ISBN 1-873203-93-4

Contents

INTRODUCTION

Making his steely-eyed entrance to reverse the ill-fortune of all present, the war film hero frequently demands, "Who is in charge here?" In real life by contrast, the question was rarely uttered; the answer was supposed to be obvious.

All officers receive a commission scroll telling them so. Mine, arriving through the official mail in a cardboard tube, gave moments of great wonderment. In it Her Majesty addressed me as *Our Trusty and well beloved*, so blinding me to more significant phrases which followed. These commanded me, to *exercise and well discipline* those placed under my orders from time to time. In turn, those subordinates were directed to obey me as *their superior Officer*.

The magnificent document's intent was perfectly clear, but whether I managed to apply it to my people in their duties was often debatable. For their part they did their very best to follow my frequently bizarre instructions if only, as in the old joke, out of curiosity. Unlike the movies, it was more often than not the circumstances which exercised command, whatever we did.

However, if all else failed, I could always read my instructions from the Queen. I have them still. Inexplicably, they are seemingly not applicable to family life.

Edward Cartner, Plymouth, 2002.

ABOUT THE AUTHOR

Edward Cartner began his working life teaching English and Physical Education. Then he applied to join the Royal Air Force and was dismayed to face a commissioning interview in Central London on New Year's morning 1964. The day was not then a National Public Holiday and so, for a Northumbrian, was a first taste of mischievous military humour. Nearly thirty years later he briefly occupied that very City office before retiring to the West Country with his wife. They have two married daughters.

I.   As Per The Book

A deal of our social training as cadets came from a little blue book full of pious advice on officers' deportment.

The volume became something of a lifeline and we were encouraged to carry it everywhere. Amongst many other topics, we could read that a degree of stiffness could be found in some messes, but that alcoholic over-indulgence and rowdyism were to be deplored.

The sensible young officer would do best to learn from his betters. Only later could a degree of informality be allowed. The youngster would do well to stand up when addressed, guard his tongue, be respectful and, above all, heed the good book.

"My, you do look handsome," said my wife when I appeared in brand-new mess dress for my first formal mess dinner. "I could fall for you."

"Just listen to this," I commanded knocking loudly on my stiff shirtfront. "It's taken me nearly fifteen minutes just to get it on."

A bus was arranged to take us from our quarters to the mess. "Now just be careful," warned my wife proudly as, stiff like a penguin, I rocked down the front path. "Just remember, you're an officer now."

She could be sure I'd be careful. The whole gleaming outfit had cost something more than a month's pay and I was loath even to sit down.

"Good evening, sir," I greeted the first person I saw on boarding.

"What ho," he replied, casually dripping cigarette ash down a crumpled sleeve. "Don't call me Sir, laddie. Not at a dinner night."

I sat in careful, but pained silence and surreptitiously fingered the little blue book in my inner pocket.

We assembled in the mess ante-room, but the book offered no way through the crowd. I knew I had to present myself to the most senior, so chose the one who appeared to have the most medals.

"Good evening, sir," I pronounced, in accordance with page 23.

"Er ... What? Oh... Yes. The CO's over there, you know."

A steward approached with a tray of delicate glasses. "There's beer if you wish, sir," and he winked towards a noisy group clustered in a corner.

"No thank you, I'll have a dry sherry, please." (As recommended on page 17.)

At the foot of the table I joined other terrified children in stiff clothes and we made low conversation in between dainty bites of largely unrecognisable food. Our older brothers-in-arms sprawled at ease amidst a litter of half-emptied wine glasses and crumpled napkins. The conversation competed with the musicians who strove to make themselves heard above the increased din, which rose further to...

As the plates were cleared and port decanters appeared, my neighbour began to squirm around a little. "What do we do if we need the gents?" he whispered urgently. These were days long before the revolutionary introduction of 'comfort breaks.'

I was suddenly glad to have kept away from the beer barrel. "Don't think we're allowed to leave the table before the CO,"

I replied, sensing the comforting pressure of the little blue book. For my part, exactly how to pass the port was the main concern. Was it to the right or the left, or even page um...?

A loud crash of the President's gavel produced immediate silence.

"Mr Vice," he bellowed, as if from Heaven. "The Queen!"

As the band produced a recognisable version of the National Anthem, in accordance with page 54, my neighbour assumed his first duty as Vice-President.

"Gentlemen," he squeaked, with legs crossed "The Queen."

All standing seized their port, intoned "The Queen," drank and sat abruptly.

I was only a half-second behind each action.

More gavel thunder introduced the President's gracious, "Gentlemen may smoke."

Stewards appeared at once with huge silver cigar boxes and fancy lighters. The musicians' gallery disappeared into a rich blue cloud base, under which we peered at each other contentedly; only the candle heat kept it above tabletop level. Shouting became the best way to communicate. Most of it came from the upper tables.

"Bloody hell," complained Mister Vice. "I'm bursting."

Then followed a bout of irreverent speeches, loud guffaws, heckling, bun-throwing and chains of tied napkins being passed over the knees. We novices joined in as best we could, but I would have to do some earnest revision as to exactly which pages authorised this mayhem.

Suddenly, we were on our feet to honour our seniors making unsteady progress towards the bar.

"Oh please hurry," moaned my nearly incontinent friend.

"Mess rugby!" somebody yelled.

I took a last lingering look at my immaculate dress: the finely pressed sleeves; the solidly starched shirtfront; real gold studs, a gift from proud parents. I would read the book tomorrow, but meanwhile…

In the ante-room we pushed a stuffed parachute ball back and forth. There were sounds of a motorbike being driven along the main corridor. The CO yelled orders, encouragement, threats and curses through a portable loudhailer. An elderly officer limped away after falling off the mantelshelf. He clutched a sooty scalp wound and two halves of his spectacles.

"Is it like this every time?" I gasped happily to my opponent as we wrestled for a broom shank under an upturned easy chair.

"Not likely," he bellowed. "We're seeing the boss off tonight. He's retiring for good. Saw the war through and everything."

In the early hours we found our discarded jackets, brushed the worst footprints off the fine cloth and consigned the unconscious war hero to an inflated rubber dinghy on a flat trolley. Quickly it was filled with fire bucket water and beer slops.

Somebody reaching down to save him from drowning inadvertently ripped off his heroic medal array and brought away the entire silk facing of the jacket.

We trundled to his house and left him parked outside the front door.

On the bus home, a hat went round for the silent driver; it probably amounted to a week's wages for him.

Somehow, I had mislaid my door keys, so had to knock gently. For reasons that escaped me – and still do – I was carrying the CO's loudhailer. "Boo!" I hollered through it, volume set to maximum. "It's me!"

The door opened abruptly and I was seized in a furious death lock.

"Be quiet!" she hissed. "I know fine well it's you." Then her eyes widened as she saw our neighbour settling down amidst the milk bottles. He had no shoes. "What will the neighbours think?" she faltered.

Well, at least I had retained all my expensive mess dress and looked down proudly at my turn-out, which had cost at least a month's pay. An immaculate shirtfront, made of what appeared to be damp brown cardboard, took pride of place.

Later I read carefully through the little blue book. There was no information at all on how to behave at real formal dinners.

With some relief, I stored it away forever. It would amuse my grandchildren one day.

II. *To Touch His Hem*

Father-figures are everywhere in military life. Sometimes we become one.

To do this we inherit appointments and titles fashioned by our predecessors, but often re-invent the wheel. During one period of administrative frustration, I demanded to know just which old duffer had written such rubbish so long before. Angrily I flipped over to the final page looking for the signature and printed name.

They were mine.

So, our own gradual transformation from wide-eyed, ineffective youngster to an operator of passable competence is subtle. There should be growing mature responsibility and fewer gross errors. If survival continues, it is said that legends then arise around that increasing service. Tales are recounted with extra stitches for each repetition until what was a snapshot of time becomes a cover-all to one's very identity.

However, there are always older heroes; the time-honoured legends. They have seen a task through from the very beginnings. They have done it all and invented many wheels. Often they rise to good rank which, combined with their deeds, ensures an honoured place in the unit history. They, or their memories, are crowded round by ambitious young officers eager to rub off some of the magic dust.

To arrive in the living presence of these gods is not easy. Their rank protects them and they surround themselves with similar high-achievers. A young lad had best observe first from a distance and only approach when he has something to contribute. It had better be good and certainly not another wheel.

In my unit there was a man of such stature. He was spoken of with affection, pride and awe. His wartime deeds coloured our early history. He was a founder figure and his influence seemed to guide the very philosophy of my immediate superiors. He was mentioned in books. There seemed to be nothing this man had not done to further the development of our work.

Just to touch his hem would be a coup for a young whipper-snapper. I could absorb the ethos by direct spiritual conduction. To sit and learn at his knee would surely guarantee eventual stardom. In turn I would inherit the mantle he bore so easily. But how?

My hero had long since submitted to the calendar of retirement from the colours, such was the Homeric description I applied to him. I learned with some disappointment that far from becoming Master of a university college, he happily passed his days as a part-time games teacher at a small prep school. Even that wisdom, I was certain, would be passed on to the boys as if from the Knights of the Round Table.

It seemed that my only hope for a passing glance, an encouraging word, a fortifying pennyworth would be to approach the presence during our annual cocktail party reception. Here we honoured our forefathers and said thank you to our customers. For we juniors it was an opportunity to impress by our social aplomb. Provided he pressed his best uniform properly and kept off the sparkling wine, a lad could do himself a lot of good on that evening.

But how to open conversation with the legend? What to say? To his hundreds of epic events I had none. I had been a baby during the War. I had no medals. Like my equally young competitors, I could offer little to interest such eminence.

Save one factor in my favour alone.

My parents came from the North East of England. Therefore, so did I. More importantly, so did The God. Most significant of all, I recalled my mother claiming that she had been a fellow athlete at the same school.

That should do it; the old-school-tie ploy, never known to fail. I could barely wait for the reception.

My moment came early and, after a couple of sundowners had stiffened my resolve, I saw the great man surrounded by my leaders. They formed a palisade of laughing court, but there was a gap and I took it boldly.

I waited, hopefully, through several moments of senior wise-cracking until noticed. He read my name badge and my rank badges and recognised me for what I was; but he was a kindly man and it was a social occasion after all.

"Hello, youngster," he said casually.

"Good evening, Sir," I began, heart a-flutter as the beams of fame shone down. "Do you remember my mother, Sir. You went to the same school."

This was the defining moment. In time, I would recall this for my own admiring successors.

He took a sip and frowned back a generation.

"Christ! I'm not your father, am I?"

III.   Need To Know

I cannot remember exactly when security measures began to play a significant part in my career. Like everybody else, however, I realised that they often add interest to a simple life.

For a short period our masters decreed that when talking to parachute dropping aircraft from the ground an irrefutable identity check should be made first. For years we had simply opened radio conversations with agreed call signs in plain words. It was peacetime, after all, and safety requirements imposed imperatives which should not be misunderstood.

Yes, yes, we were told impatiently, but you should not give the game away until you are certain to whom you speak. Only those involved need to know.

Therefore, as a trial, a cardboard code-reader was introduced which, when set to the correct date, gave two letters with which to challenge an approaching aircraft.

The respondent dialled up the same date, read your code and then replied with that displayed in the next window of his card.

That response was inserted into the original thingummy, and if it matched, a meaningful relationship could begin.

Nothing could be simpler…

Perhaps in a warm, well-lit security office it was indeed simple. However, late at night on Salisbury Plain, things could be different. Besides, the problems sometimes began long before leaving the office.

"We're still required to use the code card things," I reminded the pilot during a preliminary planning call.

"What?"

"You know. Those new slider things for identification."

"Not me, mate," the aviator claimed. "I'm a stand-in for this task. It's all news to me. Probably need-to-know anyway."

"Well, I can't give details over the phone, but surely you'll have one on board."

"Yeah, whatever you say. But you'd better have our normal call-sign just in case."

Later in my dark muddy hole on an exercise where no lights could be shown until the very last minute, I began a furtive fumbling with my now slightly limp card.

Okay, got it. Ready to transmit on time. "Authenticate Golf Alpha," I beamed out over a sizeable area of real estate.

Silence.

Eventually, and within the usual timings for these jobs, the aircraft called me.

"Drop Zone. Drop Zone. Two minutes to go."

That should have been my signal to rush around lighting a small display of flares to confirm to the approaching pilot that all was well. But not this time.

"Authenticate Golf Alpha," I insisted, all nice and laconic in accordance with the security experiment.

"Drop Zone. One minute."

I knew that the rapidly approaching twinkle of lights was my aircraft. They knew my position to within a spit. Everybody knew everything. Except, it seemed, the code.

"Nothing seen, Drop Zone," complained the pilot as he flew directly over me. "We'll go round only once more."

A light drizzle began.

'Blow the rules,' I thought. Okay, some snoop will be monitoring somewhere, but this is ludicrous.

"Look at your code card," I transmitted. "Respond to my authentication challenge, Golf Alpha. We spoke about it yesterday."

"Not me I'm afraid," came back loud and clear. "I'm a stand-in. We've got one of those card things, but it seems a bit need-to-know. Try code Victor Tango. Two minutes to go, by the way."

It was a long transmission, the baddies must have got a perfect radio fix on us.

The pilot's reply to my challenge made no sense at all until I realised that our extended chat had taken us over midnight and he had used the next day's answer.

His was the right response. It was me who was now out-of-date. But his reply should have matched my now-incorrect challenge. I was frantically looking up the new day when "One minute," came through my headphones so I rushed around lighting things.

Against a background of plain, good old-fashioned Anglo-Saxon curses, I broadcast permission to release the parachutists.

The following day I set off for another task without returning to base and in the uneasy knowledge that the wretched code-cards would continue in use. This job would also be on the first day of a new month thereby doubling the opportunity for confusion.

Our exercise was close to a tourist area in full holiday season.

"Keep things fairly tight-lipped," my boss had warned. "There's no need for the whole world to know."

On the day, my assistant and I were discussing details from behind our hands as we drove out of town.

"Maybe we should call in there and get our timings confirmed," he said.

We were passing a coach tour office where a poster proclaimed, to the exact minute, our two 'secret' drop times. A 'Mystery Tour Including Parachute Drops' was offered.

Although the dropping area was reasonably remote, a hard-top road ran alongside and we had some difficulty getting our Land Rover past the ice-cream van parked in pole position.

"Everything still on time?" called the man rubbing his hands eagerly. "Special price for you two."

Immediately before the drop, we were besieged by camera-wielding holidaymakers whose parked tour buses denied access to our troop transport. The coded identification business would have been pointless pomposity so I transmitted the necessary in plain voice.

"Looks pretty crowded down there," observed the pilot. "Everybody seems to know."

Afterwards I called into the bus company.

"Tell me," I enquired cautiously, "how were you able to time your mystery tour to include my parachute exercise so exactly."

"Ah," said the man, tapping his nose. "Now that would be telling, wouldn't it? It's all need-to-know in this game, you see."

IV.   Old Haunts

Standing before the sad, closed-down frontage of the old house I sketched a self-conscious salute just as all those years before. It was strange to return and I remembered that servicemen should never re-visit old haunts. There is nothing worse than the old boy hanging around the place, reminding the youngsters 'how things were done in my day'.

Many military sites have their ghosts. It is difficult to visit the Army's older barracks and not sense an overwhelming presence of former deeds. One RAF airfield has a phantom bomber, which makes repeated attempts at a night landing as the winter breeze sighs through the copse beside the old dispersal. "Did anybody hear that?" the orderly officer asks somewhat too casually, as he seeks company for his lonely inspection of the armoury.

Where I stood now was an old manor house, which had been a headquarters formation, disbanded at the end of my tour of duty. We had invited a visit from the elderly gentleman whose grandfather had occupied the place as a family home. Like an ephemeral breeze he wandered sadly about evoking the past and seeing ghosts invisible to us.

"This was Aunt Maude's sewing room," he said pushing open the door of what had been our post room. "She died in this house, you know."

We looked carefully at each other remembering that our ghostly bomber had been the Grey Lady seen waiting at the window overlooking the kitchen garden. *Just a trick of the light, you understand, but do you fancy a stroll while I check the bottom gate?*

Eventually only four of us remained and on the last day we raised a farewell glass to the old place, lowered the flag at the salute, locked the massive door and resolutely faced our separate futures without a backward glance.

That was usual when departing at the end of a tour of duty. Never look back. Others had already taken our place. Nobody could accuse us of comparing our times with theirs. Yet on this occasion there were no others.

We were truly the last RAF personnel and the future of the great house was unknown. Sinister patches adorned the faded walls where stirring portraits of aerial derring-do had inspired our efforts. Now they hung in other places offering new homes for our forefathers' spirits. It was a sad day; the end of a unit that boasted the longest continuous history as a Royal Air Force Headquarters.

I often wondered what became of the place, until one day my wife and I were close by and, on a whim, diverted to drive through the grounds and take a look for old time's sake.

At the front, as I saluted, the manor had a tired, dusty look and the formal gardens were obviously missing the sort of attention they had in my time. At the back, however, we were intrigued to see that the former stable block had been converted to a house.

This was entirely proper because although we had used that place only as a rather run-down garage for the commander's car, it was a listed building destined to survive whatever happened to the big house.

A man was gardening at the side and looked up warily as we approached. "Good afternoon," I began. "Sorry to appear intrusive, but I was stationed here when it was an RAF site."

The man's reaction was strangely immediate. He abandoned his work, held out his hand and insisted that we went in for tea.

"Well, that's very kind of you, but we don't want to disturb you. We only came by for a nostalgic glance."

"Think nothing of it, glad to take a break," he said. "In any case you might be able to answer a couple of questions."

We met his wife and were soon promising to send photographs of the manor in its heyday. That interested him greatly especially when we described how a pre-fabricated hut had occupied what was now his rose garden.

"The last couple of years have certainly been an interesting experience for us," he admitted ruefully. "Some times you'd swear you were being watched from the house. Must be some of those old RAF types hanging about. "

After tea our new friend mentioned that a forgotten cellar door could give us access to the house.

"But first," he said "Come and see this." He took us across to what I remembered as the old guardroom, now heavily overgrown. "In there," he gestured, "is a man's name on a board. It has haunted us since we came here. We've often wondered what became of him. The children reckon he's one of the watchers I mentioned earlier."

Just visible through the filthy window was a plastic wall-chart. The sort which at every RAF station displays in wax pencil the vital information of the day: NAAFI opening times, flag lowering roster, the duty officer.

"That officer must have been one of the last ones here," our host said. "The duty man right at the end. Have you ever come across him?"

It was a strange moment and, as I stepped back to let my wife peer in, I felt as if somehow nothing was real. The intervening years dissolved and I half expected to see the flag break out at the top of the dilapidated mast.

"Yes," I said almost in a whisper. "That was … er … is me. I was one of the last to leave. Being the junior meant permanent duty officer for the last month or two."

It seemed only fair to pull out my service identity card before his astonished gaze.

After a melancholy tour of the house the man took my hand in farewell. "I've found it quite creepy having you here," he said quietly. "Especially when we were inside."

He held on to me as I moved towards the car. "After we bought our place we became very interested in what the big house had seen over the years. That name on that board has been a sort of link."

He patted my shoulder with his free hand. "Sorry about all the touching, but I just have to make sure that you are real."

"It's a funny feeling to be taken as a ghost," I said to my wife after we had resumed our journey.

"I'm not so sure about that," she replied with a laugh, "but it's no wonder you've been a bit tired recently. The way I read that roster chart, you've been the duty officer for over fifteen years.

V. *Check, Double Check*

The power of the check-list is wondrous to behold. They can organise our lives as surely as any clock.

Shoppers use them and even the most experienced pilots. In bigger aircraft one crew member will read 'challenges' from a printed page and all others must respond correctly. Switches turned, dials noted, seat belts fastened and so on.

Some lists are plastic for wax pencil use, others scribbled on the back of the proverbial envelope; all are vital props to our scrabbling memory. Everybody uses them. Impatient young men packing for a week away should.

I wish I had…

A four-day symposium on the latest training management-speak would be a chance to acquire some new jargon. Uniform would be worn during the day, of course, but I wore that every day; who needs a list for that?

My arrival at the mess on Sunday evening coincided with that of an old acquaintance. He too would receive the wisdom, so we abandoned our luggage and resorted to the bar for some serious propping. His boisterous scepticism boded well for the way we hoped things would continue. Other fellow students joined us until, in a well-refreshed mood of 'let's see what to-morrow brings,' I returned to my room.

Unpacking my uniform produced a curious lack of shoes. Upending the case and peering under the bed made little difference. They were not there. Oh yes, I had some footwear, but not the highly-polished black version.

For a lunatic second or two I actually considered a midnight dash to fetch them from home – it was only a hundred miles or so – but a couple of hours in the bar was hardly preparation for that and the thought perished quickly.

My dilemma was resolved by an inspired stroke of genius of the sort which has authors leaping up in the middle of the night to jot down sudden brilliant ideas. My luggage did include black Cherry Blossom and yellow polishing dusters. I could convert one set of my footwear. Okay, so they wouldn't take a glossy shine, but it was only working uniform after all.

With the passionate zeal of the desperate, I took up the still-warm brown suede shoes I had been wearing all day.

Thirty minutes later I had a passable pair of black shoes; well for one o'clock in the morning, anyway.

Breakfast was the first test, but at these times messes are little different to hotels. People grope about with barely open eyes and little concern for anything other than tea and the morning paper. I quickly got my lower half hidden under a table. So far, so good.

To survive the short march to the training suite I worked myself into the centre of my group. It felt secure. Who looks at feet when passing a crowd? It is heads which count. Like the dummy in the POW escape film *Albert RN*, my outlandish shoes were secreted into the school.

It was going to be all right. Once in the study rooms, my legs would be concealed under a desk. At the first mid-morning break, I'd escape to the clothing store and buy a pair of regulation black Oxfords.

Some elements were certain and I worked through a mental checklist. A coffee break was programmed – check. The clothing store was near-by – check. I had money – double check.

It is said in the military that no plan survives first contact with the enemy, and my scheme succumbed as soon as we entered the symposium room. I should have known. We were, after all, already practised training officers, some on second or third tour of duty. We were not to sit in rows to be lectured at. It was to be a week of give and take, a period of exchanging ideas and picking over the latest ones. A formal arrangement of desks facing blackboards would be wholly unsuited for such work.

We took our seats in a single semi-circle of easy chairs.

The absurd shoes at the ends of my extended legs proclaimed my incompetence. There was nowhere else to put them. It would be most un-officer like to sit on my curled-under feet as did my wife.

"Say they're a Ministry of Defence trial," guffawed my friend. "Gotta be."

No less than the head of the training establishment bid us welcome. His succinct warmth met each of our eyes in turn with the arc of outstretched legs well below his vision. "You'll be glad to know," he concluded, "it is your brains we are interested in. This is not a course which tests deportment or turn-out." We all chuckled complacently. Actually, I thought, in this light the shoes might just pass muster. The CO turned to leave. "So saying," he continued, "I do see that at least one of you could benefit from such work."

It was obvious who would buy the drinks at the meet-and-greet that evening.

I dashed to the clothing store during the break.

Beside the serving counter was a display of priced items. They had a familiar look about them, typical of articles forgotten by careless officers. The one who neglects a check-list: ties, black socks, even a cap … and shoes.

"Good morning," I said cautiously to the corporal with as much authority as I could muster. His immediate impudent grin said it all.

My name badge announced visitor status. I was obviously in a hurry. It was the first break of a Monday morning. The man probably had a course programme in his den. Most likely he could time his queue of feckless petitioners to the second.

"And a fine good morning to you, sir," he bellowed. I wished he would keep his voice down. "And what have we forgotten today?" he went on. "Don't tell me, let me guess…"

Above his waist-high counter I passed muster easily. The last time I'd been inspected by one so junior had been at the cadet unit, but he leaned over so that no amount of pressing close to the woodwork could hide the evidence.

"Shoes!" he called happily. "Haven't had to do shoes for a while." He looked up blandly. "What size, sir?"

The shoes arrived instantly. I said no need to wrap them, but could I have the box for my ruined suedes, please?

"Do you know, sir," the NCO remarked as he wrote my receipt. " We get a new course in every week. It's amazing what you officers forget. I could set up a little side-line here selling printed check-lists."

VI.   *Could Be Tricky, Boss*

As Sergeant Wilson of *Dad's Army* often asked if the latest plan was wise, so my flight sergeant deputy had his own version. "Not sure about this one, boss; could be tricky."

I would have been foolish to ignore his caution, for his experience was vast. He was even recorded in the Guinness Book Of Records for a feat I could barely comprehend. Now he was obliged to spend a deal of his time considering the dafter ideas born of my youthful enthusiasms. Luckily for me, he remained confident that his new leader would see sense before long.

Our task was to train parachute instructors, and at his tactful suggestion I had quickly recognised that attention to detail was a major attribute to develop in our pupils.

As instructors, they would be required to examine minutely every part of the parachute, its harness and the fit of both to the parachutist. Carelessness towards their own equipment could be dangerous; the same towards that of their pupils was intolerable. One hundred percent was the minimum pass mark for safety checks.

In the early stages of the training, we could not expose real people to the sweaty fumbles of learner instructors, so these latter spent hours teaching each other the various lessons. Only towards the end of their course would we risk live bodies.

Nonetheless, I argued, it would be better to find alternative training 'fodder' for our students. "How about other members of staff?" I suggested.

"Not sure about this one, boss." The flight sergeant sucked his teeth. "Could be tricky."

"How?" I demanded desperate to learn at his knee.

"Well, the staff might try things on a bit."

"But isn't that what we want? Let the trainees work things out?"

"Still not sure."

There followed a deal of brooding over the repetitive, inward-looking nature of the early coursework until a daring innovation occurred to me.

"Got a great idea," I announced one morning. "I will act the part of an ordinary soldier parachutist. We'll build some errors into the equipment for them to find."

The flight sergeant appeared unimpressed. "But they'll know it's you and look especially carefully."

"But isn't that what we want?" This conversation was becoming repetitive.

He rubbed his chin. "Um, not sure about this one. Not too keen on my officer being made to look a fool. Could be tricky."

I could hardly pull rank, but he allowed a couple of discreet beers to clinch the deal.

At the next lesson, to a chorus of disbelieving moans and behind-hand smirks, I appeared in the line-up for a student's check. My parachute equipment was adorned with mistakes, some quite subtle, supposedly typical of novice parachutists. The session went well and afterwards even my man agreed that there might just be some value in continuing the project.

Until, that is, I suggested including more advanced errors, even to the point of actual parachuting.

There was a marked change towards a firmer, less deferential line. "Definitely not sure about that," he said. "Could be bloody dangerous for the students, as well as you. Let's be realistic."

I should have listened. After all, he was in that record book and was giving my dignity and comfort every consideration.

"That could never happen," he remarked sadly as I prepared for the next occasion, but he was too late and I presented myself for the check apparently complete in every detail. The student instructor performed well, but was very slow – he knew something must be amiss, why else would I be there – and the equipment fault I had imposed upon myself began to rub a little.

I was checked, double-checked and further inspected to the power of five. The staff instructor, not in the know on this occasion, joined in. They were extra methodical and my discomfort, like a full bladder, produced a miserable but irresistible little shuffle.

To help the lad, the flight sergeant invited me to march up and down a little way. "Might make things more obvious," he said straight-faced.

I shifted shoulder straps and hobbled about. On bending forward to ease the weight I was roundly ordered to 'stand up straight.' Things were hurting now, so I nearly forgot who I was supposed to be, and only just prevented myself turning on everybody.

Eventually, all admitted defeat and I was dismissed to totter off to my office without revealing the secret. Sometimes this pretend business could be very uncomfortable, I reflected ruefully. The flight sergeant was right – it was tricky.

A colleague came in while I was removing the harness. We had arranged to dash into town during lunch.

"Ready?" he asked. "Come on, we've only got half an hour. By the way, what's your flight sergeant on about? He said you were probably unable to walk?"

"He's right," I replied, fiddling with my laces. "One day I'll listen to sense. These boots are killing me. I've had them on the wrong feet all morning."

VII.   Get Some Time In

I missed National Service by a matter of months, but despite taking a permanent commission, always thought that the two-year compulsion would have been beneficial.

It is a curious military quirk that respect and one's spurs are often won simply by comparing lengths of service. Any callow attempt to mention one's own slight experience is often spurned by the comment, "Get some time in!"

Just when I changed from receiving this dismissal to offering it, is not clear. One early resolve, however, was that warrant officers were never to hear those words from me. Perhaps in my third decade of service I might risk a jocular reference, but only if I had known the man for years.

Junior commissioned officers, if they have any sense, listen carefully when warrants speak. Indeed, it is a warrant officer's paternal duty to instruct young officers in their deportment and only throw the lad to the wolves if he declines such counsel.

Warrant officers are addressed as Sir by all juniors and, in the Air Force, attract the honourable title of Mister from all others. They are neither NCOs nor commissioned officers. They are warrant officers, a breed apart and they have it made.

A warrant officer expects commissioned officers to behave properly with regard to public courtesies. When I was attached to an Army battalion my Company Sergeant Major, a junior warrant officer, saw nothing odd in giving me a rigid eyes right salute when walking his wife and young family one Sunday morning. To have ignored him or failed to respond would have been a gross insult. But then he knew that and also that I knew. Some time in had been acquired.

A while later I was tasked to survey a former RAF site for an exercise. The buildings were occupied by an Army unit, but the airfield was available for our use. I took along a very junior acting pilot officer who was attached to my section for familiarisation duties.

On arrival we learned that the Commanding Officer and all his commissioned officers were away, but were met at the headquarters door by the Regimental Sergeant Major, a very senior warrant officer.

"Good afternoon, sir." A quivering salute directly to me and a sidelong appraising inspection of my young attendant. "Would you care to come indoors?"

"Good afternoon. Thank you." Quietly I warned the pilot officer that eyes and ears open in total silence would serve him best.

"Do take a seat, sir," indicating a deep armchair. The youngster found himself a folding wooden contraption. "Would you like some tea?"

"That would be nice, thank you." I knew better than to rush our host on his own patch. We'd get down to business soon, but meanwhile we were like Levantine businessmen in the early stages of trading courtesy.

The RSM picked up the phone. "Brooks, get-in-here-withsome-tea-now," all in one snappy burst. How Brooks divined how many teas to deliver was a mystery.

Almost at once there was a timid knock. "I do like a cuppa at this time of day," relished the RSM. "ENTER!" My boy nearly slipped off his perch and a terrified soldier in ill-fitting overalls tip-toed in carrying a single mug.

"Excuse me, sir," grimaced the RSM as he hustled the wretch outside. Then, as if door and wall were not there, we heard explicit instructions being delivered. They appeared to concern the cleanliness of overalls, length of hair, numbers of cups and never, but never serve tea to a visiting officer *In A Mug.* "DO YOU UNDERSTAND?" we heard that part exceptionally well. The acting pilot officer quailed.

"Blimey, sir," he said. "Good job I'm a commissioned officer already."

"Don't bank on it, son. At your rank, remain alert, sit to attention and, above all, speak only when spoken to."

"Sorry about that, sir," smiled the warrant officer going behind his desk again having slammed the door on the hapless Brooks. Falling crockery noises were followed by a deep silence during which my wriggling pilot officer was subjected to contemptuous contemplation.

Another slight tap and "ENTER!" announced the final arrival of tea. In cups. On a tray. With biscuits. Naturally, the servant went at once to the most important man in the room. "You bloody fool!" snarled the RSM. "Serve the officer first!"

Way down the list, the pilot officer got his tea – no biscuit – and I explained our purpose. The survey had all been agreed in writing. My call today was courtesy only and sorry to miss the Colonel. There was no need to list further the officers' pecking order, we had been received by next-to-God anyway.

"I'll walk with you, sir," declared the RSM setting down his cup with finality. "Could do with a bit of air." The pilot officer gulped a scalding mouthful; he was learning quickly.

Like a royal progress of old, the RSM marched us – there can be no other description – towards the airfield site. On the way brief shadows made abrupt diversions into hiding, right and left. "Excuse me, sir," he would say before the slower-witted inhabitants received curt instructions on deportment and length of hair all at several yards range. I feared for the life of one who could not avoid passing close by. He knew he did not have to salute a warrant officer, but could make nothing of my RAF uniform. Nothing could save him. In the presence of the RSM, he had failed to recognise a commissioned officer.

"Will you excuse me, sir," our host took his leave graciously, "while I attend to a small discipline matter?"

I drew myself up to full military presence and thanked the gods for my previous time with the Army. My returned compliment was as immaculate as I knew how. "Of course. Thank you for your hospitality." It would have been insulting patronage to say the Colonel would hear of my satisfaction. The Colonel would expect nothing less.

"Blimey!" gasped my young escort as we watched the malefactor being marched away for several close-arrest lessons on deportment, haircuts and rank recognition. "Good job the RAF hasn't got RSM warrant officers."

"Ah well, times have changed for us. Take it all in. Look and learn, son. Get some time in."

My survey was something of an anti-climax after that and I couldn't help feeling that the young man's mind was on other things. Perhaps that single tea-party was enough to confirm his later decision that military life was not for him after all.

Many years later I sat with a houseguest. He drank my whisky. He was a serving soldier, but junior to me. I was older for a start and had seen more, but wouldn't bank on that. When we first met and he was a rising junior of few years service, he would suffer my chaffing with weary dignity. I had only one comment to his complaints of a bad day. It came with feeling from the heights of my two decades.

"Get some time in, lad."

Now in my retirement things have changed. He has been rapidly promoted several times. We remain friends. He still drinks my whisky, but I dare not suggest he needs some time. In his part of the Army he is a Regimental Sergeant Major and moreover… He is also my son-in-law.

VIII. Know Your Enemy

I am sure that my sympathy in later life for the plight of military sentries arose from a boyhood visit to London.

We had done the sights. Tower Bridge to Joe Lyon's on the Strand and next was Buckingham Palace. It was in the days when the guardsmen took post outside the railings and paced a well-polished but hazardous path through a minefield of tourists.

One immaculate soldier, his path blocked by an ignorant visitor, performed a perfect mark-time for the second or two required to clear the way. He could hardly barge the fool aside, but could not curtail his beat. It seemed to sum-up the dilemma facing all sentries. Too lax and the bad guys triumph; too hard and the passage of legitimate life comes to a halt entirely.

I remembered that palace sentry when I was involved in teaching young recruits the business of mounting guard. We reinforced our message with the old slogan 'Know Your Enemy'. It seemed to me that if that was useful to an alert sentry, then the corollary 'Know Your Friends' must be equally important.

We acknowledged the probable absence of an immediate foe. No Cossacks with snow on their boots would charge the gate, but there would be a constant passage of passers-by about their lawful occasions. Therefore, we argued, personal recognition formed the basis of good security. Certainly, salute officers, but require proof of identity if not known. Do not be bullied by senior rank. Be courteous but firm. Remember, at that stage the sentry is in charge. If in doubt, up the ante; call for help and the guard commander.

When we needed to test the youngsters' resolve, we staged an exercise during which they were instructed to stop everybody regardless. The intruders we had 'planted' then had to try their worst and play the game.

By and large things worked well. A reasonable level of security was maintained while delays at the main gate were kept to a minimum.

Early one evening I was returning to camp and, of course, expected entry under the rules we had laid down. As most of the trainees were under my command, there was a fair chance that the sentry would allow passage on personal recognition. Immediately beyond the barrier, however, a cordon of young men surrounded a car I recognised as that of my friend, James. Nearby, face to the wall was a spread-eagled figure under heavy guard.

"What's the problem?" I demanded of the sentry who had ducked under the barrier.

"Bit of an incident, sir," the lad said sternly. "Do you know that officer?"

"Yes, it looks like the Dental Officer. What's going on?"

"He's got something in his car. We've sent for the duty sergeant."

"Oh, come on, son," I raised my voice. "Everybody knows the Dental Officer. In any case I'll vouch for him."

"Who are *you*, sir?" the boy asked.

Suddenly there was a sinking feeling that I might be late to dinner.

"Listen. Let me through and I'll sort this with the corporal." I fumbled in an inner pocket for my identity card.

"Let me see your hands all the time, sir," came the courteous but firm reply.

"Okay, airman," I said resignedly. "Well done. You've all done very well. Now please will you let me through so I can talk to that officer."

"Corporal!" the boy shouted over his shoulder. "I've got another one here!"

The NCO ran across with two more guards and I was relieved to recognise him at once. He was a drill instructor from my own squadron. "Hello, sir," he saluted. "Out of the car, please. Up against the wall."

"Christ, Corps!" I demanded. "What's all this?"

"No talking, sir. Up against the wall."

James gave me a rueful grin as I assumed my star-fish shape alongside him.

"What the hell's going on? There wasn't an exercise planned for today."

"No talking," ordered a squeaky but determined voice from behind.

We became aware that they'd got the traffic moving again and just as our strained position was becoming unbearable, were ordered to turn around. The orderly sergeant had arrived. He was a flight sergeant of the RAF Regiment, another part of my squadron. I knew him well and had the greatest respect for his expertise. At that moment I fervently hoped he had similar feelings for mine.

"Good evening, sirs," he saluted gravely. "The corporal will take you into the guardroom for a couple of minutes while I have a look at the cars."

"Bloody hell, Jim … " I began inside the guardroom.

"No talking!"

The flight sergeant soon came in, dismissed the guards and invited us into an inner room.

"Well, sir," he grinned at James. "You were asking for trouble there. It's not really fair on the kids, but they were on the ball all right."

I could only gape and be none the wiser.

"Yes, flight sergeant, you're quite right. My humble apologies. The boys did well," admitted James. "I'd forgotten about having it in the car, you see."

"Okay, sir," said the NCO. "No harm done really. Probably good practice for them." He looked at me with a grin. "Just your bad luck to arrive at the wrong moment, eh?"

"Obviously, but what? Why?"

"Well, sir, to save any more embarrassment I'll leave the Dental Officer to explain in private." He fished in his smock pocket. "But here's what started it all."

He set down a highly polished hand grenade, which toppled heavily over and rolled across the table just like they do in the war movies.

James and I retired hurt to the mess, where he seemed obliged to buy the drinks. There he told me the tale.

"It was a present for my nephew... Of course, it was a harmless dummy... Trouble is, I hadn't got around to boxing it up for the boy... It was on the passenger seat..."

Rather than risk frightening the sentry, he had held it in his hand, expecting to be waved through. After all, everybody knew the Dental Officer. The trouble was that the lad was on his first ever sentry-go and was going by the book.

"There's an old saying," I said, starting on a second whisky.

"I know," he said shaking his head sorrowfully. "I'll say it for you. *With friends like this, who needs enemies!*"

IX.   *Was The Real War Like This?*

If that shadow waved again, I told myself, someone would have to go across and take a look at it. In the glimmer of early-morning streetlights, it could easily be the intruder we were there to deter.

My companion stirred uneasily, as well he might. He knew who would be sent to investigate. I had two advantages: I was the senior and more importantly, I was the one with the gun.

"Halt! Who goes there?" could be shouted in the time-honoured way. No, that was wrong. Was it, "Who's there, friend or foe?"

I would just have to get out my special card, which listed the correct words, and memorise them all over again.

That card was the cause of my present predicament. It not only instructed all anxious sentries in their duties, but also proclaimed my qualification to bear arms. In the best films, the CO grabs any old machine-gun and blazes away at the dive-bombers. In real life, only qualified and in-practice personnel can carry weapons.

My commanding officer this night was an embarrassed technical sergeant with a length of perimeter fence to guard. He was dismayed to find himself leading a bunch of staff officers, all strangers to each other, and of which only the most senior could legally be given a rifle. He had our sympathies, but it was his problem and while he argued with his masters, I obeyed the last order and guarded my tree. Some things never change, of course, and the rifle, with its awkward angles, became as heavy as ever was, and the ground remained cold and hard. Moreover, just what, I asked myself, were we doing here anyway?

It was all very strange. For years everybody knew that the real job for RAF HQ staff was to pace the floor while the boys took the fight to the foe. Our commander would look like Jack

Hawkins or Richard Todd and there would be a sorrowing Labrador somewhere.

As for ground defence? Well, we had the Army didn't we?

That's how it was meant to be. Just like the cinema.

That image had to change, of course, and by the mid-seventies distinct signs of all of us being in the same defensive boat emerged. Teams of examiners were appointed to arrive without notice and test preparedness.

It was not long before these eagle-eyed snoops became The Enemy, not Herman Goering anymore, or the Soviet Spetznas, or even the usual run of headquarters management inspectors. It seemed that just to satisfy the testers had become our primary aim.

As part of a large HQ, doomed to fly desks and shuffle paper, we all worked in tight-knit cells with little neighbourly contact. When a defence exercise was called, each sector found itself manned by an unlikely bunch of warriors, all ignorant of the grand plan. Those whose qualification card was valid, as was mine from a previous appointment, took on a value beyond their worth.

That's why I was squinting at tree shadows that night, but it gave food for thought.

On a previous tour of duty my unit had provided a squad to respond quickly to any emergency on the station. Proper combat clothing was not then available so the team turned out in their usual RAF clothing.

Their leader was from a different section and also lacked official accoutrement. Being a keen young officer, however, he had bought an Audie Murphy outfit from the nearest Army Surplus Store.

I attended the first deployment as a neutral observer.

"Morning, sir!" He snapped off a John Wayne salute. "Where are my troops?"

"Well, that's for you to solve?" The men, all well known to me, awaited orders over a pack of cards in a nearby minibus.

The lad bounded over. "Right, chaps," he ordered. "Fall in out here!"

A reluctant posse of bored NCOs climbed out and formed up. The boy soldier saw their unwarlike dress at once. He took a heroic pose, legs apart, arms akimbo.

"Look at me," he ordered. "Why can't you be like me?"

I took the young man aside.

"Look, son," I began. "At best their role is unclear and they've no proper kit. They don't know you and even if they did, you'd need to wear the same badge to get any results at all."

At the end of the exercise I took the senior man aside.

"Now look," I said sternly. "That young officer was doing his best, so let's have an end to it. Just what was the problem?"

"Well, sir, it's all so daft."

I saw his point some weeks later when observing a party practising perimeter control. A bunch of 'rioters' had been recruited to create a disturbance as if demanding illegal entry to the station. The young guard commander had closed the gates and formed his team behind in a show of calm determination.

Insults, clods of earth and small pebbles rained down upon us. After a few menacing minutes everything came to a halt to allow the local bread van access with the daily rations. Then a group of mums arrived with their tots for the crèche.

The rioters' growing boredom was definitely favouring the defenders until a fire hose was brought out on our side. 'To wash down the entry area', they said. In less than a minute, the nozzle was snatched through the bars by the enemy.

We endured several minutes of cold lashing rain before my opposite number beyond the gate restored order and called a halt. At that point, the real guard corporal emerged from his warm lair.

"Just a thought, sir," he observed. "Did you know the tap was on our side all along?"

Perhaps guarding this tree was not so bad after all. Little responsibility and it was dry. Nevertheless, when this was all over I would call on my uncle who had served man and boy, war and peace.

"Tell me," I would ask naively, "was the real war like this?"

X.   *Never, But Never Again*

For the second time in an hour, I failed to lift my feet high enough. The yacht's bow wave combined neatly with the lumpy sea and now both my boots were full.

'What,' I asked myself, 'am I doing here?' Why, in my mid-forties, am I sitting on the hard edge of a large sailing boat, wellies over the side, in the company of ten other dummies?

It had all begun innocently enough. An invitation to join the racing crew of one of Her Majesty's training yachts; a simple enough prospect, involving an overnight thrash to Guernsey for a prize presentation followed by a party, then a lazy day in harbour. After that, I was assured, we could take a couple of days to work the boat back to England.

I could hardly refuse; sailing had been an obsession since boyhood. I knew the skipper well and had voyaged many hundreds of miles as his deputy on the same vessel. True, I had a couple of doubts about racing again after years of cruising and training trips, but we could pool our experience and win the day for the RAF against the Navy and the Army.

When the crew mustered just before departure, we were one person short so the skipper went recruiting along the pontoons. He soon returned with a large amiable young man whose tattoo proclaimed him a Royal Marine.

"This is Mick," our leader announced. "He couldn't get a place on the Navy yacht."

"Done much sailing, Mick?" I asked.

"Nope, this is a first for me."

"Show Mick the ropes," the skipper instructed after we had made a reasonable start, "so he'll know what's what when we get out to sea." That moment was nearly upon us as the yacht bowled along with a good heel likely to last the day.

Given that 'showing the ropes' might take in anything from astro-navigation to reef knots, it seemed best only to show our beginner how to wind ropes onto a winch and then restrict his duties to that.

My careful demonstration came to nought when Mick casually took hold of the straining rope and, by-passing the drum completely, fastened it directly.

"When do we eat?" he asked, scarcely out of breath.

By now we were clearing the land and the skipper insisted on a show of boots along the rail as seen on all the best yacht-racing photos. We all dutifully lined up, except Mick who was retained as muscle-power in the cockpit. Military rank was always discounted on those boats, but it was odd how I had to take my place right at the front. It was something to do with being one of only two commissioned officers in the crew – and ensured that I broke the spray's force for everybody else. I took a death-grip on the forward lower shroud, which thrummed like a suspension bridge carrying rush-hour traffic. One of my dangling wellies filled with cold English Channel almost immediately.

"What are we doing here?" I grumbled to the other officer who sat next to me. He too had given up racing years before.

"It's good character-forming stuff, they say," he said and ducked behind my shoulder as another tidal wave swept the foredeck.

"Any chance of any grub?" we heard the Royal Marine shout.

"Hear, hear!" I yelled. "It's cold and wet and hungry up here. Get the kettle on!"

"Okay, you wimps!" bawled the skipper. "Mick's going to sort a meal now."

The lad was sent down to delve into our tinned military rations. It would be a simple business of opening a can each of stew, heating the lot and serving with chunks of bread all washed down with Sergeant Major Tea: 10 tea-bags, condensed milk, 4 sugars. That's the stuff to feed the troops.

Unfortunately, another first for Mick was seasickness and soon all he could do was grab any old thing, whip off the lid and pass it up to the masses.

Slowly a line of tins made its way hand-over-hand to our exposed position beside the mast. At last... food.

"It's hardly silver service, is it?" remarked my friend. "And this meal is decidedly under-cooked." He tipped a dry sample into my hand.

"Better share with mine," I offered. "It's good character-building stuff." Quickly we worked out how to dip first into my tin then his. Surprising how many rice grains will stick onto strawberry-jam fingers.

It was a full two hours before the skipper relented and allowed us off the deck. Thankfully, the off-watch gang stumbled below and we heard welcome sounds of the kettle. "I feel better now," remarked Mick. "I'm bloody starving."

"Honestly," I protested to the skipper. "Just what were we doing up there?"

"It's a race," he replied crossly. "Need to keep the boat upright."

"But she weighs 25 tons!" I cried. "And it's blowing hard."

"It's good for the soul. You cruising people have it soft. Get your head down now, I want you on the wheel when we approach the islands. It'll be dark then."

"Christ, I'm hungry." It was the Marines again.

Late on the following morning we moored at St Peter Port with just enough time to tidy-up and have a shower before the prize-giving. We had done well and took second place in our division.

"Great," we said collectively, "all is forgiven." Now would come a damned good meal, a few beers and an easy Sunday in harbour before taking our ship back home.

Our skipper collected the runner-up medal, but was strangely reluctant to join the celebration.

"Sorry, lads," he announced sheepishly. "Things have changed. Got to get the boat back for Monday morning. She's due an inspection. We'll just catch the tide."

"I know exactly what you're going to say," my wife warned when I arrived home at Sunday midnight. "You've said it before after sailing on those boats."

"Yes, I know," I admitted. "But this time I mean it. I'm never going on those Government yachts again. Never."

Funny how time changes things. Only a few weeks later I was boarding the very same vessel again for a week-long training voyage for novices.

You see, they needed an experienced, uncomplaining officer whose character was already well-formed.

How could I refuse?

XI. *Like It Ought To Be*

Sometimes so many minor hiccups affect a programme that it seems best just to abandon the plan and think again.

We were hosting a parachuting group from one of our allied partners. Their be-medalled pedigree made us blink a little, but we were determined to demonstrate a similar level of professional expertise. My overall responsibility included programme planning, but as my staff we were doing that all the time, I had no fears. Affairs would proceed smoothly.

An early hint of trouble-in-store came on the first day. Our visitors, travelling in their own bus from the airport, were taken to a nearby station. The driver, realising their nationality, had made an assumption and, of course, the visitors knew no better until arrival. We were drumming our fingers with puzzled impatience when my deputy took a call.

"Hey, are you guys expecting a bunch of paratroopers?" our neighbours asked. "We got 'em here."

It was only 15 miles away, so they had lunch before resuming their journey.

The following day we roused everybody before dawn to beat a borderline weather forecast. Our aircraft arrived on time and quickly loaded for the first of what was meant to be three rapidly repeated sorties. That was trouble-free and we hurried everybody back by road. So far, so good.

The CO joined me in Operations for a progress report.

"I was surprised to hear you'd gone for the early morning," he began. "Especially on last night's forecast."

"Well, it paid off," I said. "And the second's just got going."

"Er, sorry, Boss," the operations staff interrupted. "We've just heard. They've abandoned in the air. Engine snag. He's returning to his base with the troops on board."

It was mid-afternoon before I heard that the aircraft could not be fixed, there was no spare available and that coaches had been sent to bring the troops home. It was only 25 miles, but they would be given high tea over there.

Then the promised poor weather arrived. The boss limited his comments to one terse sentence.

"It ought not to be like this, you know."

The third day was the old, old story. Desperately clutching at weather straws in between showing our visitors archive film and yarning in the coffee bar. By teatime we had achieved nothing and run out of film.

"Tomorrow, Saturday, will be okay for you all day," advised the weatherman. "It is June, after all."

"Problem is," said my planning officer, "we haven't got an aircraft. It's been diverted to a higher priority."

I could have taken a bet on the CO's words. "I know it's not your fault," he said, "but it ought not to be like this."

"Okay," I announced to everybody. "Plan B. We'll each take a visitor as a personal guest for the weekend."

My man, Gordon, looked as if he'd visited everywhere in the World as well as serving two tours of combat duty. I offered him Oxford, despite misgivings over weekend traffic chaos and only knowing the place as an occasional family shopping destination.

" Great," said Gordon. "Anywhere's fine, this is my first time in England."

When we arrived in the city, I was still mourning the loss of our parachuting programme and found it strangely difficulty to see the place through the eyes of a first-time visitor.

I need not have concerned myself; Gordon was delighted.

"Will you look at that! I've seen that in a book," he enthused pointing his camera and stepping back off the pavement to focus. "It's just... Aw, thanks," he said as I heaved him back to safety. "Guess I forgot you guys drive on the wrong side of the road."

The river was thronged with undergraduates in striped blazers and straw boaters punting with their girls. Rowing eights sped up and down. I could scarcely believe my own eyes.

"Jesus!" invoked Gordon. "Are those guys real? I guess they're shooting a movie, right?"

"No, they're real enough," I said modestly as if this was just another stage in a well-laid plan. "Look, over there's a cricket match." On the other bank, framed by trees in full leaf and on vivid green, was a cricket match all in white. It resembled a perfect still life of Ye Olde England. I certainly was getting to grips with this tourist guide business.

"Don't tell me how the game is played," Gordon insisted. "I'll take it through the skin like you guys. It's just ... Hey!" he shouted suddenly, "One of those players moved just now. Is that allowed?"

Over everything ruled a cloudless sky and brilliant sunshine. Slight zephyrs of warm breeze ruffled the water. It was a perfect day for parachuting.

"So what's the most English thing in this town?" my guest demanded happily after we'd completed a full circuit.

"Well, there's a famous marmalade shop just up there," I pointed.

"Marmalade! Can you really buy that stuff?"

The shop was empty, but for two blonde assistants, all cut-glass Chelsea tones and crisp white pinafores. I introduced Gordon and left him to conduct his own defence.

After a short while he floated out, carrying a large wicker basket brim-full of jars. "Gee," he whispered. "Those accents! Sure hope the folks back home like marmalade."

I had suggested to the CO that we meet at a typical English tavern for lunch. To enter my choice we had to inch down a narrow passage lined by tottering stacks of beer kegs and mouldy cardboard boxes. Inside was a dim bar with a tobacco smoke cloud at shoulder height. There was real sawdust on the floor.

"Sorry about this," I said. "It's the first time I've been in here."

"Jesus," Gordon breathed reverentially through the gloom, "I gotta book about places like this. Do they serve that warm beer here?"

The CO and his guest were already in place. "Where on earth did you hear about this place?" he demanded taking me aside. "It's a disgraceful place to bring visitors. We had to squeeze past some dustbins just to get in. It ought not to be like this, you know…"

Meanwhile the two visitors greeted each other excitedly.

"Did you see those dudes in the striped vests? Weren't they something? And that cricket!" Gordon exclaimed.

"I'm sorry about the weather," the boss broke in, as if needing to distract attention from our surroundings. "It's a pity we didn't have this yesterday."

"Sure," Gordon shrugged casually. "We lost a couple, but we can jump any time. Who cares? This Ox-Ford is the place to be. Real Brits in real England… just like it oughtta be!"

XII. *Affix Stamp Here*

From my deep armchair, slippered feet lost in the carpet pile, it was hard to believe I was leading an advisory party to a distant land just south of Sumatra, a recent purchaser of British parachutes, our mission to offer the benefit of our experience to the eager new users.

Proudly, I looked around at my team as they struggled manfully to occupy the Club Class cabin of the Jumbo Jet. It would be a long flight, but eight Oriental air hostesses giving only three of us 14 hours attention promised to dull the pain.

In my passport, an impressive visa filled a whole page. Translation was unnecessary, the awesome impact of the rubber stamp alone had transformed us into an instrument of policy.

During a solemn, but largely incomprehensible Whitehall briefing I had been advised that our purpose was unprecedented. 'There will be a deal of playing things by ear and we don't really know where in the jungle you will actually be...' To cover this anxious possibility, our baggage included a bulky collection of machetes, water-purifying pills and mosquito-proof bivouac tents.

Nevertheless, it would be a wonderful opportunity to operate with our hosts and to share their procedures. We could learn from each other – that's what everybody does – so my preparations had included formal permission from my masters to fly and parachute with them. This took the form of a signal; a 'flimsy' – a single, closely-typed sheet.

It was a military telegram. Verbs, pronouns and other bits of gracious grammar were omitted in the interest of brevity. Only the essentials appeared. These allowed me and Tom (my deputy) to do what we asked. To the dismay of Paul, the junior and a non-parachutist, he could be trained out there and jump with us. It was all in the name of demonstrating our confidence in the equipment. Needless to say, Paul quickly acquired his personal copy of such treachery.

I had rarely owned a document of such muscle.

The country enjoyed a military regime – or at least their army did – so we were met on arrival by a tough-looking squad of fully armed soldiery, each wearing a differently coloured beret. Ignoring the Customs and Immigration queue, they swept us to a luxurious air-conditioned people carrier. Baggage would follow, sign language informed us, and they crammed into a jeep-like vehicle to lead the way.

We spread ourselves over the dozen or so seats available and tried conversation with our driver, who first opened every window. The heat crushed us immediately.

"Ingliss…" he said, charging at right angles towards a line of stalled traffic. "Gooood."

"Er, yes. We are English," I replied, eyes tight shut as if concentrating on translation.

We swerved wildly behind a hand-drawn cart laden with heavily stuffed plastic sacks.

"Christ!" cried Tom. "Not many trees yet, boss," he added.

"Gooood. Ingliss. Ingliss," confirmed our driver. With the speedometer indicating eighty somethings, he waved both hands and joined a six-lane modern highway. We passed our grinning Keystone Cops escort. "Ingliss!" came their cry like a password.

A jungle of traffic, clogged boulevards and high-rise blocks closed around us. The animals honked and shunted at each other angrily. After a while, we pulled into a clearing in front of a huge many-starred hotel.

"Not much call for the mosquito nets then, boss," observed Tom dryly.

Our first week confirmed the London warning on lack of information. We attended briefings with all manner of senior officers. In every case, we offered our help and co-operation, but were returned to the hotel swimming pool to await instructions. Things would happen 'soooon.' It was arduous jungle living, right enough.

Early in the second week, I learned that only one jump was planned and mentioned that in Britain even qualified parachutists converted on more than that. A period of horse-trading began.

"Who you?" A non-jumping brigadier from their headquarters demanded. He was friendly, but it hardly sounded that way. "Why you here? What you do? How you tell me what do?" My handy-for-the-pocket book of diplomacy was not coping at all until he too abruptly ran out of foreign phrases. "Okay, no problem. We do you say. How many?"

I held up five fingers. He countered with three. We settled on four.

"Our government says, please may we jump with you," I said, producing my magic paperwork.

"Who jump? Where your government?"

"In London," and I passed over the document. Two colonels joined us to pore over the paper.

"No good," they said. "Where permit?"

"This is it," I offered. "My government says okay to jump, if you agree. They accept risk. They take responsibility for me and my men." I gestured around towards Tom and Paul who had gravitated towards the cool drinks away from the high politics.

'Everything under control, Boss?' Tom signalled with his eyebrows.

"Okay," said the brigadier suddenly. "Major Didi go English Embassy. Get permit."

Gosh, I thought, was it only a week ago since I'd reported there on arrival?

Major Didi was a special forces major, sporting a low-slung automatic pistol and a rainbow of assorted badges, one of which had been awarded by my own hand the previous year when he completed a course in England.

"Okay, Eddard. No problem . We fix. You come."

Tom and Paul were banished to more cold beer and swimming pool duty while Didi led a sweaty march to the nearby British Embassy. To cross the road he simply stepped off the pavement into the frantic traffic, so causing immediate screeching brakes and countless minor bumps. It must have been that cannon he had strapped to his hip, although I did learn later that officers in uniform took priority everywhere.

That counted for nothing with the British embassy receptionist, who was a cool English rose. "Good afternoon, gentlemen. Please take your pistol off. Can I help?"

"Good afternoon," I began with deep gratitude. "Can we make an appointment to…"

"Me spik," commanded Didi, laying his Colt on the desk. A long burnished knife followed. "We see Attaché now pliss."

"Have you an appointment?"

"May I explain what this is about," I began. The Rose looked surprised, as if she'd just realised I was English. "You see…"

"Me spik. We see Attaché. Most important."

Inexplicably, the receptionist offered sudden surrender.

"Of course…" and picked up an internal phone. She must have spotted some more of Didi's armoury.

The Military Attaché was a relaxed cavalry colonel who received us with impeccable courtesy. I saluted him with precision. He offered tea. I accepted gratefully. Didi abruptly refused for us both.

"Me spik Ingliss now," and in truth his range was good, but English to English explanations might have been clearer. Eventually, Didi produced my signal of authority for us to jump. "No good," he said. "Not correct."

The colonel read the paper carefully.

"Yes ... I see. Well, I must say it all seems in order to me. Why anybody would want to do such a thing is a different matter. But the intent of my Government is perfectly clear." Then, as far as I could tell, he repeated this in Didi's language.

"No good. See. Not stamp by Ingliss."

"Oh," exclaimed my saviour, "is that all?" He picked up his phone. "James, bring in the big stamp, please."

The deputy Attaché came in immediately with a large circular rubber stamp. He applied it with reverence to my document where it left a vivid red Royal Coat of Arms, easily the diameter of a teacup.

Didi was transformed. Beams, handshakes and protestations of goodwill accompanied our hasty departure. I mourned for the tea. At the front entrance, my re-armed escort hurried me into a jeep.

"Now no problem, Eddard," he smiled. "We go my government. Get okay copy."

While I prepared to meet more officialdom at yet another government location, the calm of the British Embassy garden gave way to the chaos all around. Suddenly we spun into a thronged alley and pulled up outside a nondescript shopfront. 'Fuji', it called itself, in the international language of commerce. As in a spy film, I told myself, the final authority for our unprecedented intent would be granted in a high-tech secret department masquerading as a photo-booth.

Didi rushed in, waving my precious document and set the attendant to immediate work. He quickly emerged, brandishing a sheaf of copies – the secret bunker was just a copy shop after all.

"Is OK. No problem. Now you parachute me. Ingliss, goood."

I grinned back at him and give a thumbs-up. Soon I would receive some instructions and could prise my team off the poolside.

"Very good. *Bagus*," I offered from my phrase book. "*Sekarang abri payung*."

"Didi looked baffled. "Who you say army?"

"No problem," I laughed.

I was being optimistic again. Didi fastened the papers into a clip on the dash, but the car failed to start and, as we consulted under the bonnet, a monsoon rainstorm fell onto us in our open-topped vehicle.

Sadly, I watched the Lion and the Unicorn bleed as the precious paperwork soaked to pulp.

Somewhere in the hotel, I hoped, Paul still had his copy.

XIII. Airborne! – All The Way, Sir

Centrally, in the 'Home of the British Army' flew the Royal Air Force sky-blue ensign. Surrounded on all sides by Her Majesty's dark green forces it proudly proclaimed that here sanity could be found.

For a full and exciting tour of duty I commanded the small unit, our role to provide specialist parachute instructor support to the Airborne Forces. Naturally, we owed unswerving allegiance to the RAF, but when one's daily commander is a

Red Beret brigadier and the Air Force masters are some 80 miles away, pragmatism must rule.

One day the brigade commander arrived unannounced. He knew us well and came regularly for his own training, but today he had greater things in mind.

"White coffee, one sugar, please," he said courteously to my hovering clerk. Then, "I think I need a special favour from the Blue Jobs this week," he began mischievously.

I cleared my mind of immediate worries such as whether we had enough decent biscuits left and came to wary alertness. Was I being set-up for something?

"How are things with you all?" he continued.

" Okay, Sir. This calm weather's helping."

"I bet. My people tell me you've got a balloon working this week."

The boss was referring to one of our frequent parachuting programmes from a tethered gas-filled balloon. It sounds prehistoric now, but in the late eighties such jumping platforms provided routine training and had done so for over forty years.

"Yes, indeed, Sir," I said with some relief. "I'll have you included on a date to suit."

"Alas, not for me, but I would be glad if you could help out with a visitor." He sipped his coffee and grinned at me.

74

I knew it was a set-up. Why else would the Commander come down in person? His staff had failed to convince mine about something. They wanted to give some old veteran a nostalgic jump. It was a set-up, I knew it.

We could indulge our green brothers' gung-ho enthusiasms only so far. They were much to my taste anyway, but 'rules is rules' and, eventually, we had to impose the rigorous standards of peacetime parachute training. That was my job. That's why we were there. I carried that particular can.

Naturally, a few months absence of close supervision could produce some cavalier interpretations of the regulations. Therefore, to cover my tracks, I made regular visits to my real boss at the distant RAF station to tell him what we were up to. This had mixed benefit for both of us and occasionally I got the distinct impression that he'd rather not know.

The brigadier outlined the plan. The visitor was an American 3-star General; equivalent to a lieutenant general of the British Army and, Lord help me, an air marshal of the RAF.

"Should be all right," he said. "It's an official visit, of course, but he's ex-Airborne and has always wanted to jump from our balloon. Your HQ people seem happy. Sounds OK to you?"

'Christ,' I thought, 'a 3-star has to be fifty at least'.

"When did he last jump, sir?" I asked, as casually as possible.

"About six months ago apparently. He's very keen and keeps fit."

The boss was making ready-to-leave movements and I'd already used up my quick-thinking allowance. "Okay, Sir, but he must do some preliminary training with us."

"I thought you'd say that … Agreed."

As he drove off, the Commander wound down his window. "By the way, include the general's staff as well. Thanks for the coffee."

My deputy was less generous about the general's potential. "Christ, boss!" he groaned. "A 3-star's got to be pushing sixty. And what about his staff?"

On the day, however, most fears evaporated when the general arrived. He bounded out of their bus with buoyant eagerness. "Okay, let's go! Airborne!" he cried.

"Airborne! All the way, Sir!" echoed his equally punchy staff officers.

All that is, save two. The first was a British Army cavalry major, whose regiment probably pre-dated the entire United States. He was a liaison officer for the general's time in England and made his feelings plain from the start.

"My dear boy, this is certainly not what I had in mind at all. I think you're all raving lunatics. And as for being in the RAF as well, I just don't know."

We struck him off the jumping list. The relief was mutual.

The other less-than-enthusiastic backer of the call-to-arms was an American lieutenant colonel. We put his preoccupation down to unfamiliar straps and buckles.

"Okay!" cried the chief, after the statutory training. "That's great, young fella," he bawled at me. "Let's go jump balloon!"

"Right on, sir," bawled his men. "Airborne!" The colonel's shout was probably lost in the fuss of boarding the coach.

The following morning my brigade commander phoned to say thanks for fixing and congratulations on a slick programme. The general was delighted. He thought the British Army was great and, "Gee, Brigadier those crazy Air Force guys you got with you. Just great." They'd all got two jumps. Nothing could be finer. Airborne all the way.

I passed on the plaudits to my warrant officer, who had supervised the parachuting. "No probs, boss," he admitted modestly. "One of the Americans only jumped once, mind."

"Oh, was he injured first time?"

"Not exactly. He wasn't very keen, but we persuaded him in the end. Unusual for an American, he didn't have many badges up. Not even jump wings. Funny that."

In near panic I rang the brigadier's Chief of Staff.

"Hey, I thought that American party were all parachutists!"

"Really? Didn't you know? There was the British major, of course, then that half-colonel, he's not a jumper. Not qualified. Congratulations, by the way. The Commander's delighted. You're the blue-eyed boy this week."

I opened the list of things to tell my far-away boss next week. Sadly, I deleted my note about the American general and his ruffy-tuffy staff. It would have been a nice little feather in my cap, but now it seemed best not mention that.

Best lie low for a while.

XIV. *Just Routine*

It was hard to believe that they were really going to do it – close an international airport at the height of the late holiday season so that we could drop parachutists all over it.

A routine signal eventually confirmed the task, its format no different from any other received by my unit every day. It was the usual go-ahead from headquarters giving dates, aircraft numbers, location, exact time and the like, just another job in a busy month.

The plan had provoked a series of preliminary meetings and at one of these I had looked for early confirmation.

"Are you sure this can be done?" I asked the Airport Director with some disbelief.

"Oh yes," he replied calmly, "but you'll need to stick strictly to the time slot. Other than that, we would be delighted if the Airborne Forces would join our 50th birthday celebrations. A parachute drop would be a perfect illustration of the historic links between us."

So the airport would be closed. All I had to do was to prepare a parachute landing area and supervise the drop. It would be best if the parachutists missed the very expensive aircraft and even better if they were not hoovered up by the giant engines… and there was a deal of hard tarmac… and the show must be easily visible to all… and… and…

I tried to allay these little worries by asking a string of oblique questions.

"I suppose you couldn't clear the place of Jumbos completely?"

"No not really, but you'll get 40 minutes of no activity on our part."

"I imagine a few pairs of descending size tens could do a bit of harm to a Boeing."

"Yes," said the Director casually. "I imagine they could. I'll just have to retain complete faith in your expertise."

I tried not to think what a Jumbo cost.

Then there was the extraordinary experience of pacing out the intended ground surrounded by taxiing aircraft with rows of faces peering out. Eventually I convinced myself that enough room could just be found between the myriad free-standing electrical panels, reinforced concrete and sharp light standards. On one side a broad runway to the sun, on the other, a staff car park and a fire station.

The final plan was to have our leading aircraft drop free-fall parachutists and be followed within minutes by three – Christ three! – dropping troops at low level. The free fallers would use agile, steerable parachutes and could pick their spot to land, but for the low-level men it was something else; they couldn't steer and had little control over their destination. Endless anxious re-calculation of my drift figures proved that we'd be OK – just – provided there was no crosswind.

When I arrived with a small team on the day it seemed windy. This was confirmed by the airport control tower. "Sixteen knots," they reported from their sheltered lair. A Boeing 747 trundled past; its wingtip seemed to pass directly over our heads. The din was damaging.

'Bloody hell!' I thought. 'Already three knots above the limit for clear ground, and a crosswind into the bargain.'

"But signs of dropping…" the tower added.

As I considered my trust in their word, an elegant, brass-buttoned aide came across; all polished leather and self-importance.

"Who's in charge here?" he sneered. Clearly, he had little understanding of the RAF and cared less for my many worries.

"That's me," I shouted crossly above the racket, as our last near-miss howled down the runway. 'I outrank you, Lieutenant,' I thought, 'and could do without this.'

He sketched an insolent salute, but I wasn't going to find fault; already my first aircraft was calling from some miles away. We had entered our 'period of grace'. The great airport fell silent, as if holding its breath. The man was unabashed.

"I am to instruct you, from the General, that the drop will take place."

My intended succinct invitation as to what he could do with his instructions was diverted by a second, more urgent radio call. The pilot wanted to know how things were with us down there. I translated his professional jargon for my clerk who, wide-eyed, had been brought along to maintain a written record. If necessary, it would become my life raft. I had a bad feeling about this task.

After the free-fall had taken three circuits of precious time to perfect, I transmitted 'clear to drop' for the approaching low-level trio. The clerk recorded a wind speed of 13 knots – spot on the upper limit, honestly.

Roars of approval from the assembled Army brass and delayed holidaymakers greeted the skyful of troops. Fervently I willed them all to land away from the runway, the cars, the waiting Jumbos. Please land right on me. I was almost pointing to the spot. Most of them did, but for one group who just had to scatter themselves across the concrete, the car park and the fire station.

Despite continued ecstatic applause from the terminal area, I decided to call a halt while we appeared to be winning. Honour had been satisfied and the aircraft were instructed to land with their remaining troops. In any case, the wind had risen again – honestly.

While counting heads and checking cars for dents, we saw a parachute draped over the fire station roof. The jumper's anguished cries tore at my conscience and I rushed across in a frenzy.

He had collided with the rubber, knock-aside door of the place and was suspended at about 10 feet. He was making no effort to free himself. He must have horrific injuries.

"Fetch the ambulance!" I yelled.

"Camera! Camera!" he bellowed. "For Christ sakes somebody bring a camera! This is one for the album!"

There was little to do after that. No serious injuries were reported and, when I heard that the Press was out in force, I declined to attend the reception. We had meat pies and tea with the excited paratroopers and drove home.

In the morning the telephone began a ceaseless clamour. My RAF masters appeared anxious about something. Threatening reference to unauthorised display was made. I would be required to attend and answer some stern questions. By contrast, my Army commander was cock-a-hoop.

"Well done indeed for yesterday! Difficult decision. Lots of pressure, but a great show in the end."

I was savouring his every word when my deputy came in with a sheaf of morning papers. "Have you seen these, Boss?"

The headlines told it all.

'Celebration blown off course', yelled *The Times*.

There was a picture of the injured man 'clinging' to the airport fire station and reference to the needless, extreme risk of it all.

Suddenly, I was regretting that it was my clerk's day off. He had the diary notes, my liferaft.

I still had a bad feeling about this task…

XV. Leading From The Front

"The trouble with young men like you," remarked one of my early commanding officers, "is that you're so 'hands-on' you all get killed in the first charge."

I could hardly deny his point. 'Never ask the men to do what you wouldn't do yourself' had become part of my creed.

"Stand back a bit more," he advised. "Engage brain before anything else." He gave me a direct look and picked up a sheaf of papers; it was his confidential report on my performance. The interview was over and I was moving to a new appointment.

At least, I consoled myself, it would be an active role with plenty of charging to do. Many of my new colleagues thought the same and we quickly convinced ourselves that our behaviour was good for the chaps. Let them see real leadership in action. After their sheltered years at university they were entering the hard world of directed endeavour. Who better to show the way than us? We were only slightly older, anyway.

One day the Deputy Commandant announced that the standard of student behaviour in the mess was not good enough. The place was not an undergraduate common-room. Although wearing officers' uniform, the young men were not yet 'real'. Some wise direction was required.

The training programme did not include structured training in social matters but, he said, the solution was obvious and simple…

As a start, therefore, we younger staff officers were to sit amongst the youngsters at the formal dinner that very evening. By 'leading from the front' we could discreetly impose guidance and order. It was what they wanted anyway.

The meal was notable for slower service and therefore colder food when compared to our usual places 'above the salt'. Similarly, the conversation all around was conducted in an incomprehensible undergraduate jargon. It was hard to believe that had been my language less than ten years previously.

After a while my dining neighbour announced that all he wanted to do was fly aeroplanes and could see little point in 'all this other nonsense.'

"And, by the way," he continued, "just what are you lot doing down this end of the table? We don't want you here, you know."

A year or two later I was posted to a station where my squadron formed a reaction squad during unit exercises. Their job was to attend any incident, repel or arrest the bad guys and secure the perimeter. It was ideal employment for a gang of fit, gung-ho young men whose primary role in RAF life was quite daring anyway.

I was their leader in real life, but during war games acted simply as a sort of observer. A 'top cover' referee called upon to resolve any ambiguities in their role-play. I was obliged to 'stand back' and make informed judgement while the boys scampered about the place in response to real or imagined threats.

Early one morning after an exercise night shift I had a couple of hours to kill before breakfast, after which I would be about my normal duties. It was an ideal opportunity to mingle with my men. Show willing. Share the pain. Not require them to do anything I would not do myself … It was all in the creed.

I should have got my head down followed by a shave and clean shirt ready for the new day. Instead I found myself fully kitted, buckled and armed, jogging noisily along a rutted track in an uncertain dawn of pouring rain. It was exemplary leading from the front.

I puffed alongside the front trooper, a character well-known to me.

"How's it going?" I gasped. "Have you had anything to eat yet?" All proper concern for the chaps' welfare.

My man, barely out of breath, gave the matter some thought. "You know where I'd be if I was an officer?" He nodded towards the distant office block. "I'd be in there, drawing arrows on a map. What the hell, boss…" he continued, in baffled tones, "just what the hell are you doing here?"

Towards the end of my career I commanded an active unit populated by another gang of fit, gung-ho young men much of whose work included flying as rear crew in large aircraft on parachute dropping sorties.

Although my officer duties required a detailed knowledge of the flying task, my usual work was back at base. However, as leadership style never changes, it was hardly surprising that to lead from the front, not require the men to… etc, made flying with them unavoidable.

By being listed as an assistant, I was careful never to assume command of a team, but rather left that element to the experts. Even so, I did have to attain a satisfactory level of expertise in what was a 'junior', albeit demanding duty. I convinced myself that the boys were happy with this arrangement and to have a bit of senior rank around did, on occasion, help them in any arguments at the aircraft base.

We flew by day and night, when ninety fully-equipped parachutists took every inch of the big aircraft's cargo space. To describe the conditions as a cattle-truck is to imply that we had plenty of room.

Not far off the ground we bucked and swayed about. Seats had to be lifted and secured. Heavy bags of equipment distributed to each soldier and, above all, an eye kept on the clock. Not to be ready at the drop time was the ultimate sin.

It was more important, however, to subject every man to a detailed close check of his parachute equipment. It was my peoples' responsibility and therefore when I flew, mine.

We squeezed intimately between the packed soldiery while the aircraft continued its weaving dance. Time was always running out, but we were practised and had done it many times before.

One night, with minutes to go and during my last check, the soldier grunted an apology – at least I think it was – and at six inches range presented the contents of his stomach.

The warm bolus caught my sweaty bare chest just above the 'v' of my overall and trickled down to all parts.

We got the troops out and I was left alone with a roll of paper towel. After a while, the senior sergeant came back, grinning and holding his nose in an exaggerated manner.

"Okay now, boss?" he bellowed. "You're, right. Sometimes, it is good to have an officer up here with us!"

XVI. *Your Teeth Are Here, Sir*

I once knew a helicopter pilot who so baffled ground control-lers with his heavy North Country tones that he was sent for elocution training. Soon the improved version took to the air again. Ground control was even more confused, but, as he was a brilliant pilot, agreed that they would change – or listen more carefully.

Clear statements of intent are essential for military efficiency, especially when dealing across the boundaries of specialisation. When talking to other branches of the Service it pays to communicate without ambiguity.

Take dental officers for example…

By and large, I enjoyed robust health throughout my service. All systems seemed to thrive on the sort of treatment my life meted out. All that is, but my teeth.

I joined the officer cadet unit with an impressive dental history. Most of my devastating manly smile had been lost on the playing fields of England in the name of school and college rugby. Natural teeth, never much good anyway, had given way to artifice.

Innocently, I had imagined that if not actually suffering toothache, the Service would just let things be, but that was never so. Certified dental fitness was essential for a continued career and I quickly formed intimate relationships with successive dental officers. They could not be faulted. My communication, however, left much to be desired.

My first RAF dentist remained calm.

"My goodness," he muttered after a long poke about. "How old did you say you were?"

"Aaargh," I replied as respectfully as is possible with a mouthful of surgical steel. He was, after all, senior to me. As a cadet, everybody was.

"No need to say sir every time," he advised.

His good work was ruined only weeks later when a railway porter closed the door on my curly pipe. I was leaning out to bid stiff-upper-lip farewell to my bride and, in my mind, was off to the Front again. The heroic pose was totally destroyed by a frantic grovelling for the glowing tobacco ball in my trouser turn-ups while simultaneously gagging to avoid swallowing the broken dental crown.

"Oh, Lord," the dental officer said. "Back so soon? What appears to be the trouble?"

"Aaargh – plurgg." I was beginning to extend the conversation.

Later, when I began to fly as part of my duties, I was alarmed to learn that trapped air in a filling could expand at altitude and cause exquisite pain. Naturally, I imagined my head exploding on the next sortie. However, the treatment continued to be first-class and included being fitted with sufficient gold to make me attractive to any self-respecting bullion thief.

"These should do the trick," the dentist remarked proudly.

"Aaargh – plurgg – urrgg," I agreed.

Increasing age, and possibly seniority in rank, seemed to slow the decline of my gnashers and the regular appointments became less drastic. Some social intercourse, as between officers of the same mess, became possible.

"How's your family these days?" The dental officer would ask kindly.

"Aaargh – plurgg – O levels – glurrg – nearly." My, how good it was to exchange news with friends.

"I see, how interesting. Well, not much to do today."

After two decades of this, it came as a delicious irony that my younger daughter chose to become a dentist. I tried all ways to convince her that only military dental officers had the life of Riley. Exciting red-blooded patients, all kit provided and, best for me, her expenses paid through university.

She'd have none of it. Most extraordinary; I'd yet to let her look in my mouth. Perhaps her mother had been talking.

However, I was able to tap one friendship on her behalf. This was the last dental officer to do major work on me and whose craft I carry to this day. Could he, I asked, get some teeth for the girl? Apparently, student dentists stick them into turnips or something and then practice drilling. It seemed only yesterday I'd been giving her a knuckle to chew.

"Too easy," he said. "I'd be delighted. Extracted teeth are just discarded usually. Leave it with me for a day or two."

I had uneasy visions of him calling in extra patients to deprive them of their molars. It was, after all, the first time in our friendship that I'd managed intelligible remarks about dentistry.

He contacted me at the Army unit where I was serving. "All fixed. I've spoken to the colonel at your garrison dental centre. He's an old chum of mine. Your teeth will be ready next week."

"Good morning," I announced myself on collection day. "I've come to collect some teeth."

My RAF uniform seemed to fluster the receptionist. "Yes, sir," she said nervously fluttering through some record cards. "Who did them for you?"

Did them? Did what? I asked myself. Then, "I believe it was the colonel."

"Oh dear. The colonel's not here today, but the major can see you at once."

Before I could dig my way out of this latest hole, a very large man appeared. He looked like the front-row forward who had taken my smile in the first place. He wore a white coat and major's badges.

"This officer's come for his teeth," the woman began. "But Colonel… "

"No worries. Come on through. I'll have a quick dekko. Soon fix you up."

In an instant I was propelled into his chair. "Just a minute… Aaargh – plurrg!"

From the corner of my eye I saw the nurse thumbing through a fistful of plastic bags containing dentures and things. "Nothing for the RAF here," she mused.

"That's funny," said the major. "You've already got a very good set. When were you in?"

As they puzzled over this strange Air Force behaviour, the receptionist came in. She rattled a brimming jam jar like a maraca. "I suddenly remembered where the colonel had put your teeth, sir. Here they are."

I seized my trophy and turned to flee.

"Funny people, these RAF types," the major began to the nurse. "Sometimes you'd swear they spoke a different language."

XVII. *It's The Generation Gap*

There is an RAF story of a Vulcan bomber squadron commander who flew in turn with all his newly-qualified co-pilots. It was, he told himself, good for the kids. They would learn at his knee and he could form a fair judgement.

One day, the wing commander, strapped in on stand-by, began the get-to-know-you routine with his latest victim. Within seconds it transpired, amongst other things, that the youngster had been born on the very day his boss was commissioned.

Sadly, the great man concluded, edging his bifocals out of sight, it sounded like time to move on.

Everything had changed in the young pup's favour. Things were not at all like the old days when we served under the oft-repeated mantra, "If it was good enough for me, young man, then it's good enough for you."

By the time I acquired young officers to chase around, baffling management techniques had arrived: see the youngsters' point of view; get the best out of them by inspired leadership, heavily coated with earnest welfare considerations; discuss the task in hand; seek their opinion; understand and respect their perspective; be modern, man…

Easier said than done. Under the pressure of trying to fit two day's work into one, the more subtle measures were often submerged in a series of laconic orders which brooked no argument. Luckily, most juniors were just as likely to become keen, loyal professionals as we had been. They just expressed things differently, but I did miss some of the deference we had been obliged to display.

So saying, there was a time when the combined specialist experience of my three junior officers totalled less than two years. We were a busy unit and could carry no passengers, so I enjoyed an extended period of sleepless nights. Our Army customers expected a faultless performance on each occasion and had little sympathy. Besides, they had young pups of their own to worry about.

At an early stage of this period, I protested to my commanding unit about the lack of experience.

"Well," came the reply, "we imagine you'll give on-the-job training."

"Of course," I argued. "But if we have four jobs on together, gentle introduction becomes difficult."

"I see," said the man who had made the appointments. "Maybe it's a generation gap thing. Remember what we were like. They'll be okay in time."

I returned to my unit, seething and muttering dark threats about desk-bound wallahs who had no conception of what we were up against – *them* up at headquarters. I wailed inwardly in the time-honoured manner of all coal-face workers, and in so doing I conveniently forgot that only months before I had handed over that very job to my tormentor.

Back at the front line I received a call from the pilot of an aircraft task from the day before.

"Well, it went okay in the end," he said.

I knew him quite well and realised that he was being diplomatic. "In the end? What do you mean, in the end?"

"Just as well it was a gin-clear day," he continued obliquely. "So it didn't really matter … in the end."

"What didn't matter!" I yelled, frantically scanning the operations log to see which of my officers had been on that job. A name jumped out at me. It was the most disorganised and casual of my young Turks. My shoulders sagged.

"The ground signal letter was upside-down," my caller continued. "Good job the boss wasn't on board. It was only stores anyway. Just thought you ought to know."

There was no immediate target for my rage, as everybody was deployed to a big exercise in the North of England. I was due to drive up there that afternoon to assess how well the other young men had learned their business, but now the upside-down miscreant took centre stage. He would have to shadow me – and learn.

He made one mistake during the next two days and that affected only him. By reading British Summer Time rather than the required GMT, he gave himself a lonely hour deep in the midnight hills. It was no big thing; everybody does that sooner or later. Why, even I was once presented with a cardboard Mickey Mouse clock by sniggering students after an identical error.

Nevertheless, after the successful completion of our part, I decided to take him back south in my car. We could share the driving and, like the Vulcan pilot, I could pass on the benefit of my years. As an up-to-date 'touchy-feely' leader, I might even allow him the odd point of view.

There would be no escape for my captive audience during the long journey. I began with a gentle rehearsal of my expectations of him as an officer under my command. Nothing too old-fashioned, just a subtle reminder of the old principles: see to the horses first, then the men and then maybe, oneself.

Then there had been the occasions when his time keeping had been somewhat awry. On one day actually non-existent when he'd forgotten to note a weekend roster and gone on a date. Luckily, but unknown to him, the task had been cancelled late on the Friday. And there was the matter of the upside-down signal…

"I was hoping you'd not hear about that, boss," he admitted.

"Well, it was the aircraft captain who told me."

"It's a bit silly, I suppose," he said, just a touch too lightly for my taste. "But I'd forgotten my compass. I was only a hundred and eighty degrees out. In the right place, though."

We cleared the air with an academic consideration of the ground rules. Later, I was relieved to see that he was a fine driver, and we passed the final hour or so in pleasant inconsequential chat and dozing.

Eventually, I asked him if he thought I'd been fair. Had my criticism been appropriate? Was there anything else he wished to discuss? It was all good stuff, straight from the latest lexicon of man-management-speak.

"Great," he replied without hesitation. "I'm gripping this job now. Things look good. No outstanding probs."

On arrival at base I shook his hand, man-to-man, eye-to-eye. "Okay then?" I said with some relief. "No hard feelings. Fresh start on Monday. Enjoy your weekend." It was good to be a modern mentor with a sense of humour.

"Yeah great stuff, boss. See you Monday."

He grinned and turned to go.

"Maybe I should mention… I lost my pistol last week."

XVIII. I'm In Command Today

When I took my wife to the railway station I realised that because my CO was also away, I could enjoy a double helping of unquestioned leadership: for the day, temporary command of the station; in the evening, the home.

"Have a nice day at the office, dear," she laughed.

I returned to the camp in a mood of optimistic anticipation.

My secretary greeted me with a reminder that one of the regular inspections was due. I would go to the medical centre, take a cup of coffee from my doctor friend and between expressions of medical woe, complete a surprise check on the regulated drugs stock. Count the pills, sign the register, have another cup of coffee. Nobody had said that being a station commander was easy.

"The medical officer is off sick," the PA announced cautiously. "So the civvy locum is in."

"In that case, forget it."

"Ah," she confessed. "I was getting your diary organised and sort-of gave the medics just a hint that a check was due."

My vision of a day free of all supervision, RAF and matrimonial, was fading quickly. It was only mid-morning and already I was under control again. Still, I could hardly blame her; she had previously saved me from many a forgetful moment.

"Okay," I said briskly. "Run me through the programme again and let's get going."

"Right, sir," she replied happily, brandishing a closely-typed page. "It's very light, actually. Drugs check now, then lunch with the High Sheriff. Meet in the mess at twelve-thirty."

"Okay. Sounds good, thank you."

Nothing to it, really. I'm in command.

"Good morning, sir," boomed the medical admin clerk who was clearly not taken by surprise at all. "I'll let the doc know you're here."

I'd not met the locum before, but he seemed relaxed enough and only attended the check because the book said he had to. The clerk handled the register and the multitude of keys required to open the drugs cabinet.

Various bottles were produced. We did random pill counts in a flat funnel thing. Only a few fell on the floor.

"What are these for?" I asked after struggling to pronounce an incomprehensible Latin-sounding name. "One hundred and twenty five, by the way."

"Oh, they're a tranquilliser," said the doctor in a bored sort of way.

"And these?"

"Another tranquilliser. Different symptoms, you know."

Three more bottles taught me more instantly-forgotten Latin and that the cupboard seemed the most serene place on the unit, and I said so.

"Yes," said the doc. "I suppose it's a sign of the times in a way. They're very effective."

"Well I must say," and I grinned at the clerk who, under the stress of the inspection, appeared to need one of his pills immediately, "I get most of my tranquillity from a tall bottle be-hind the bar."

Clearly, it was the wrong thing to say. The doctor straightened his back and then, under the approving gaze of his assistant, delivered a concise, but stern lecture on the evils of alcohol; especially for those in command.

Chastened, I retreated to my highly polished car and driver. I didn't get a cup of coffee either.

As we took our places for the formal lunch, the hitherto silent Mrs High Sheriff casually whispered in my ear that she was vegetarian. She could not contemplate the moulded pate delicacy, however perfectly presented. Further, she was not looking forward to the red-meat course, which took pride of place on the beautifully embossed menu card.

"Do excuse me a moment," I offered, as calmly as I could. "I am expecting an urgent message and I see that the steward has it."

He and I had an urgent consultation, which chiefly comprised angry frowns on my part and rolling eyes on his. To my relief and without discernible delay, a single non-meat plate was served as immaculately as ever and the lady tucked in without a qualm.

Back at my office, I challenged the PA. "I thought we always did a diet check for these civic visitors. What happened this time?"

"But we did, sir and here's the written confirmation from the City office. No special dietary consideration."

Things were beyond my control again and the first part of my intended quiet afternoon was passed apologising to the chef. "No problems, boss," he said generously as we split a left-over bottle of wine. "After a few years in this game you learn to be ready for anything."

Then I received an urgent call to attend on the heating engineer at my quarter. He was there to introduce what appeared to be a new idea – a working gas boiler. I had promised my wife summer-dress conditions when she returned.

The kitchen was littered with boiler bits.

"Doesn't look good," the tooth-sucking expert began. "The house is too big for the system. Doesn't look good at all…"

"The hot water tank's leaking as well," I reported.

"Doesn't look good. I'll have to turn it off completely and come back with a new bit."

"But it's the middle of February!"

"No problem about parts," he said packing his tools. "I'll be back tomorrow."

'So will my wife and the CO,' I thought miserably, and returned to the office.

Dinner in the mess seemed a better option than baked beans over the gas fire. Besides, it would be good for the youngsters to dine with the great man. There was nothing on television anyway.

During my bath, courtesy of the electric immersion heater, I contemplated once again the bell-push above the taps, a relic of the good old days when a single ring would have summoned a batman to scrub one's back and offer fresh towels. Ah, those were times to be a commanding officer, a real lord of all they surveyed.

At the mess, a junior officer had brought a girlfriend in for dinner and I graciously joined them at the table.

"Hello," I said to the lad, in the modern manner and looked expectantly towards his companion. In the old days, the entire place would have jumped to its feet when the CO, even the acting one, came in. Of course, in the early Nineties that was not going to happen, but a reasonably formal introduction was on the cards.

"Hello, boss," he replied easily and turned towards the woman. "This one's a nice old boy," he said, as she held out her hand.

I met my wife the following afternoon.

"Was it good being in charge?" she asked, innocently. "Everybody running around for you and all that?"

XIX. *Look To Your Front!*

It was only after I had been accepted for RAF officer training that the old soldiers' warnings came to mind. Bull. Burnishing fire buckets to bright metal only to paint them red again. Polishing already gleaming floors with toothbrushes. Above all, they cautioned, beware the Drill Pig... endless 'square-bashing.'

Oddly, for a supposedly ill-disciplined college boy, I came to enjoy foot drill at the cadet unit. It matched my recent gymnastic training, I suppose – bodily movement requiring co-ordination, precision and co-operation.

We learned the meaning of one command early.

"Look to your front!" the flight sergeant would snarl as we craned to see what trouble had fallen onto some hapless colleague along the rank. It would be our turn next, like as not.

However, under the press of life in the 'real' Air Force, drill just became a minor drop of many years of water under the bridge. Until, that is, I was appointed to a post where freedom parades and colour hoisting ceremonies took a major role.

The commanding officer developed a taste for standing on a dais to receive the salute of his troops as they marched to breakfast. 'Strange how life turns out,' I would reflect, while awaiting his pleasure as the men shivered behind me in a winter gale straight off the Bristol Channel. My more technical colleagues would scuttle past to their warm computer suites, eyes averted as if to avoid being drawn in to this anachronistic pantomime.

In time, I was released from this duty, but could not deny the satisfaction of having led my troops through the Bank Holiday streets of a West Country holiday resort. Bayonets Fixed, Drums Beating and Flags Flying, as proclaimed by the municipal scroll which granted us the privilege.

Whether the system then took notice of these acquired skills I knew not, but my last station appointment saw me planning from my senior desk, a grand parade as Freemen of our borough. 50 years to the day, we would celebrate our unit's formation. Bayonets would be fixed, drums would beat and flags would fly. I would not march this time, but knew that any default would be carried in my can.

The Mayor would, of course, review the parade and I went to brief him. He was doubtless an able politician and became a good friend, but was not military. After we had gone through a series of timings and traffic matters, I sought to explain how the parade commander would salute him with a sword. The Mayor had already burdened himself with a few new worries.

"You mentioned inspection earlier. Do I actually have to inspect the men? What do I look for?"

"Well, not exactly, sir. It's ceremonial. Just appear to look at each man as you pass."

"Oh dear," he worried. "Won't they be embarrassed?"

"No, not really. They're used to it and will look to their front. You can stop for a word or two with the odd one."

"Oh dear. What do I say?"

"Well, you can ask where they come from. How long they've been in the RAF. That sort of thing."

"Oh dear."

"Now, sir," I said, trying to return to essentials. "When any officer on the parade faces you and points his sword at the ground, you raise your hat. It's a salute and…"

"Hat?" said the Mayor.

His secretary chipped in. "We're a new borough. There's no mayor's hat."

It was my turn. "Oh dear. Well, strictly speaking, a hat should be worn."

"Oh dear. What sort of hat?"

"Usually it's a black bowler."

"Oh dear."

How they got a Mayor's hat, I never discovered, but they did. It was indeed a black bowler and it was raised perfectly whenever any officer as much as hinted at the ground with his sword point.

Well before the great day, however, I was to face new tests of foot drill knowledge.

Naturally, there were many rehearsals. Nothing in the military can take place without rehearsal – sometimes even the rehearsals are rehearsed – and we would be no different.

For the final one, the dress occasion at which I would play the Mayor's part, my mercurial commander came up with a wizard wheeze. "Have you got a big wide hat? A Panama?"

"Er, yes…" It was a long-served veteran, now resembling a tired hay bale.

"Great! Wear it. Raid your wife's jewellery box for a chain to go round your shoulders just like the Mayor will have."

"But…"

"No problem. It'll steady the men. Give them a chance before they see the real thing. If they can keep looking to their front with that, they'll have no problems on the day."

And so on a warm summer's evening we paraded the fully-armed troops in their best uniforms. The pretend mayor's car drew up to the saluting dais. The pretend mayor, in dark City suit, fragile old straw hat and the longest of his wife's golden chains, stepped out. The real Station Commander saluted, straight of face.

The Parade Commander approached. His sword pointed to the ground. The Panama, shedding the odd wisp, survived the first of much doffing. I pursed my lips and glared at my friend, forbidding him to laugh. His lower face remained impassive, twinkling eyes well shadowed under the peak of his cap.

"Parade ready for your inspection, Sir," he spluttered.

The first squad's flight sergeant turned nary a hair, but I could just imagine the scandalised thoughts of the other NCOs. Bloody Officers! My passing brought a ripple of surreptitious twitching in the first rank of immaculate youngsters until a muttered, but not-to-be-denied growl came from the rear.

"Look to your front!"

XX.   *Keeping Ahead of the Game*

Every junior officer dreams of the day when he commands his own unit. After a long apprenticeship it will be an opportunity to impress one's personality on the place and be in control of events. At last he will be ahead of the game.

Eventually, and much to my surprise and delight, a command was offered to me. It was a tiny place, and instead of aircraft and runways, had boats and jetties. No matter, the important thing was that it was mine. Remaining sensitive to well-established routine, I could introduce improvement and lead from the front.

My first two months were to demonstrate how that would never be allowed.

An early call was on the Lord Mayor for me to say hello and my predecessor farewell. After only a few moments of polite chit-chat the Mace Bearer, in his ever-present role of body-guard, took firm command.

"Aye," he queried. "Is the sun over the yard-arm yet?"

In mid-sentence the Lord Mayor leapt to his feet anxiously and peered through the window.

"Yes, I do believe it is. If you say so."

"Aye," declared the Mace Man, producing a decanter of whisky.

"Don't worry," muttered my colleague. "This happens all the time. He's been with 15 previous Lord Mayors."

I took a sly look at my watch. "But it's only half-past two in the afternoon," I protested weakly.

"You can't change local custom. Just enjoy it."

Shortly afterwards the same Lord Mayor paid an official visit to my station. It was an important opportunity to demonstrate the full range of our activity, most of which I had only recently grasped myself.

Preparation of the programme gave a fine opening to flex my personality muscles. "Let's make it informative but relaxed," I instructed my deputy. "In particular allow enough time for the Lord Mayor to chat to the junior ranks."

The Mace Bearer came along too, of course. "Aye, Station Commander," he declared. "Things have changed a bit hereabouts." Later I discovered that he had served his final RAF years at the station and was wont to make comparison. Once the Lord Mayor was involved in his programme the Mace Bearer embarked on a private inspection of the place. "Just seeing how things are going."

It seemed best just to appoint a shadow, so leaving us to concentrate on the senior visitor. This worked well until the Lord Mayor, coffee in hand with a group of fascinated juniors, was interrupted by his guardian's sudden re-appearance. "Aye, Station Commander," came the dramatic announcement. "The Lord Mayor will make his departure now." The limousine arrived, the Mayor was hustled into it and I appeared to be the only person surprised.

"We seemed to miss a biggish chunk of the programme," I remarked to my second-in-command.

"Fraid so, " he agreed. "It always happens. The Mace Bearer keeps the Mayors ahead of the game all right."

Soon came a series of Christmas affairs including an informal dinner party in the mess. I intended that my role as host would be enlivened by it being my birthday. "But don't worry," I announced to the family. "Everything will be okay. I command here. We'll be well ahead of the game."

It was a fine meal in excellent company. One of my junior officers excelled himself by falling off the piano. The noise from his bagpipes hardly changed at all, but, as my daughter noted, he did reveal exactly what was worn under the kilt. In keeping with the new regime's ethos, I got discreet word around that celebrations for a select few would continue at the Station Commander's Residence.

I appeared to command more elite than I knew and had been unable to prevent the piper receiving the invitation. He led the way with a stirring march only fifty percent unrecognisable. My wife fretted about how much bacon she had for the traditional early-morning fry-up and I pondered the identity of the stout gent busily chatting-up my daughter's friend.

At home we banished the bagpiper to the lounge where he competed with an LP record at full volume of the Argyle and Sutherland Highlanders. Luckily, it was a big house so only odd snatches reached the kitchen. The mystery guest turned out to be one of the resident weathermen, so that was all right. I was in full command again.

"I think you should come into the hall," our daughter advised. "That weatherman's fallen down the cellar stairs with a pile of bread and butter." We rushed out, expecting broken limbs, only to find the wretched man peeling our midnight feast off his elbows and knees. Wearily, my wife set to work again.

"It's all right," I said. "He's got most of it on the plate again. He says his dinner jacket was dry-cleaned only last week."

The following afternoon was wild and blustery so we took a short drive to enjoy the coastal scenery. On return, the sentry seemed very excited. "Hello, sir, ma'am!" he yelled raising the barrier and eyeing up our twenty-one-year old in the back. "It's all been happening here. Helicopters! The whole lot!"

Nothing seemed different in the immediate vicinity.

"Who's in charge?" I asked with thudding heart.

"It's all at the officers' mess," the lad continued happily. "Blankets, ambulances. Everything."

We expected to find the mess collapsed to rubble at least, but my deputy appeared, tired, but relaxed. "No problems, boss," he assured me. "They've had some food and we've got a bed each for them. The High Commission is sending somebody down."

"But who? What?" I spluttered.

"Hasn't anybody told you? A ship sunk this afternoon and all the survivors were brought here. You weren't around, so I said okay. It's the most exciting thing that's happened here for years. Good job we were ahead of the game with blankets and things."

Within a few days my hopes of calm command suffered another blow. After a very stormy day, I suggested that we drive down to the shore to see the high tide. It was dark and we took our second car, a battered, but loyal old Mini.

Rounding the last sloping bend, the car drowned itself in a tidal surge, which unexpectedly swept up from the quay. Not far away, the main stores building stood knee-deep in water.

Opening the Mini doors completed the flooding and we stepped out into what was to become a busy night.

I allowed myself one consolation as we squelched wetly up the hill to alert the duty staff. By being first at the scene, I was, for the first time since assuming command, ahead of the game.

Also published by Woodfield...

The following titles are all available in high-quality softback format

RAF HUMOUR

Bawdy Ballads & Dirty Ditties of the RAF – A huge collection of the bawdy songs and rude recitations beloved by RAF personnel in WW2. Certain to amuse any RAF veteran. Uncensored – so strictly adults only! *"Not for the frail, the fraightfully posh or proper gels – but great fun for everyone else!"* **£9.95**

Upside Down Nothing on the Clock – Dozens of jokes and anecdotes contributed by RAF personnel from AC2s to the top brass... still one of our best sellers. *"Highly enjoyable."* **£6.00**

Upside Down Again! – Our second great collection of RAF jokes, funny stories and anecdotes – a great gift for those with a high-flying sense of humour! *"Very funny indeed."* **£6.00**

Was It Like This For You? – A feast of humorous reminiscences & cartoons depicting the more comical aspects of life in the RAF. *"Will bring back many happy memories. Highly recommended."* **£6.00**

MILITARY MEMOIRS & HISTORIES – THE POST-WAR PERIOD

Flying the Waves Richard Pike describes his eventful second career as a commercial helicpter pilot, which involved coastguard Air/Sea Rescue operations in the Shetlands and North Sea. **£9.95**

From Port T to RAF Gan The history of the RAF's most deserted outpost is comprehensively and entertainingly charted by **Peter Doling**, a former RAF officer who served on Gan in the 1970s. Many photos, some in colour. **£14.95**

I Have Control... Former RAF Parachute instructor **Edward Cartner** humorously recalls the many mishaps, blunders and faux-pas of his military career. *Superb writing; very amusing indeed.* **£9.95**

Korea: We Lived They Died Former soldier with Duke of Wellington's Regt **Alan Carter** reveals the appalling truth of front-line life for British troops in this now forgotten war. *Very funny in places too.* **£9.95**

Meteor Eject! Former 257 Sqn pilot [1950s] **Nick Carter** recalls the early days of RAF jets and his many adventures flying Meteors, including one very lucky escape via a Mk.2 Martin-Baker ejector seat... **£9.95**

Pluck Under Fire Eventful Korean War experiences of **John Pluck** with the Middlesex Regiment. **£9.95**

Return to Gan Michael Butler's light-hearted account of life at RAF Gan in 1960 and the founding of 'Radio Gan'. *Will delight those who also served at this remote RAF outpost in the Indian Ocean.* **£12.00**

The Spice of Flight Former RAF pilot **Richard Pike** delivers a fascinating account of flying Lightnings, Phantoms and later helicopters with 56, 43(F) & 19 Sqns in the RAF of the 1960s & 70s. **£9.95**

Tread Lightly into Danger Bomb-disposal expert **Anthony Charlwood**'s experiences in some of the world's most dangerous hotspots (Kuwait, Iraq, Lebanon, Somalia, etc) over the last 30 years. **£9.95**

Who is in Charge Here...? Former RAF Parachute instructor **Edward Cartner** regales us with more inglorious moments from the latter part of his military career as a senior officer. *Superb writing; very amusing indeed.* **£9.95**

MILITARY MEMOIRS & HISTORIES – WORLD WAR 1 & 2

2297: A POW's Story Taken prisoner at Dunkirk, **John Lawrence** spent 5 years as a POW at Lamsdorf, Jagendorf, Posen and elsewhere. *"A very interesting & delightfully illustrated account of his experiences."* **£6.00**

A Bird Over Berlin Former Lancaster pilot with 61 Sqn, **Tony Bird DFC** tells a remarkable tale of survival against the odds during raids on the German capital & as a POW. *"An incredible-but-true sequence of events."* **£9.95**

A Journey from Blandford The wartime exploits of motorcycle dispatch rider **B.A. Jones** began at Blandford Camp in Dorset but took him to Dunkirk, the Middle East, D-Day and beyond... **£9.95**

A Lighter Shade of Blue A former Radar Operator **Reg O'Neil** recalls his WW2 service in Malta and Italy with 16004 AMES – a front-line mobile radar unit. *'Interesting, informative and amusing.'* **£9.95**

A Shilling's Worth of Promises Delightfully funny memoirs of **Fred Hitchcock,** recalling his years as an RAF airman during the war and later amusing escapades in the UK and Egypt. *A very entertaining read.* **£9.95**

Beaufighters BOAC & Me – WW2 Beaufighter navigator **Sam Wright** served a full tour with 254 Sqn and was later seconded to BOAC on early postwar overseas routes. *'Captures the spirit of the Beaufighter'* **£9.95**

Coastal Command Pilot Former Hudson pilot **Ted Rayner's** outstanding account of his unusual WW2 Coastal Command experiences, flying in the Arctic from bases in Iceland and Greenland. **£9.95**

Cyril Wild: The Tall Man Who Never Slept – **James Bradley's** biography of a remarkable Japanese-speaking British Army officer who helped many POWs survive on the infamous Burma railway. **£9.95**

Desert War Diary by **John Walton** Diary and photos recording the activities of the Hurricanes and personnel of 213 Squadron during WW2 in Cyprus and Egypt. *"Informative and entertaining."* **£9.95**

From Fiji to Balkan Skies Spitfire/Mustang pilot **Dennis McCaig** recalls eventful WW2 operations over the Adriatic/Balkans with 249 Sqn in 43/44. *'A rip-roaring real-life adventure, splendidly written.'* **£9.95**

From Horses to Chieftains – Long-serving Army veteran **Richard Napier** recalls an eventful Army career that began with a cavalry regiment in 1935; took in El Alamein & D-Day and ended in the 1960s. **£9.95**

Get Some In! The many wartime adventures of **Mervyn Base**, a WW2 RAF Bomb Disposal expert **£9.95**

Just a Survivor Former Lancaster navigator **Phil Potts** tells his remarkable tale of survival against the odds in the air with 103 Sqn and later as a POW. *'An enlightening and well written account.'* **£9.95**

Memoirs of a 'Goldfish' • The eventful wartime memoirs of former 115 Sqn Wellington pilot **Jim Burtt-Smith**, now president of the Goldfish Club - exclusively for aviators who have force-landed into water. **£9.95**

Nobody Unprepared – The history of No 78 Sqn RAF is told in full for the first time by **Vernon Holland** in this absorbing account of the Whitley/Halifax squadron's World War 2 exploits. Full statistics and roll of honour. **£14.95**

No Brylcreem, No Medals – RAF MT driver **Jack Hambleton** 's splendid account of his wartime escapades in England, Shetlands & Middle East blends comic/tragic aspects of war in uniquely entertaining way. **£9.95**

Nobody's Hero • Former RAF Policeman **Bernard Hart-Hallam's** extraordinary adventures with 2TAF Security Section on D-Day and beyond in France, Belgium & Germany. *"Unique and frequently surprising."* **£9.95**

Once a Cameron Highlander • This biog of Robert Burns, who, at 104 was the oldest survivor of the Battle of the Somme; takes in his WW1 experiences, later life in showbusiness and celebrity status as a centenarian. **£9.95**

Operation Pharos • **Ken Rosam** tells the story of the RAF's secret bomber base/staging post on the Cocos Keeling islands during WW2 and of many operations from there. *'A fascinating slice of RAF history.'* **£9.95**

Over Hell & High Water • WW2 navigator **Les Parsons** survived 31 ops on Lancasters with 622 Sqn, then went on to fly Liberators in Far East with 99 Sqn. *'An exceptional tale of 'double jeopardy'.* **£9.95**

Pacifist to Glider Pilot • The son of Plymouth Brethren parents, **Alec Waldron** renounced their pacifism and went on to pilot gliders with the Glider Pilot Regiment at both Sicily & Arnhem. *Excellent photos.* **£9.95**

Pathfinder Force Balkans • Pathfinder F/Engineer **Geoff Curtis** saw action over Germany & Italy before baling out over Hungary. He was a POW in Komarno, Stalags 17a & 17b. *'An amazing catalogue of adventures.'* **£9.95**

Per Ardua Pro Patria • Humour and tragedy are interwoven in these unassuming autobiographical observations of **Dennis Wiltshire**, a former Lancaster Flight Engineer who later worked for NASA. **£9.95**

Ploughs, Planes & Palliasses • Entertaining recollections of RAF pilot **Percy Carruthers**, who flew Baltimores in Egypt with 223 Squadron and was later a POW at Stalag Luft 1 & 6. **£9.95**

RAF/UXB The Story of RAF Bomb Disposal • Stories contributed by wartime RAF BD veterans that will surprise and educate the uninitiated. *"Amazing stories of very brave men."* **£9.95**

Railway to Runway • Wartime diary & letters of Halifax Observer **Leslie Harris** – killed in action with 76 Sqn in 1943 – poignantly capture the spirit of the wartime RAF in the words of a 20-year-old airman. **£9.95**

Seletar Crowning Glory • The history of the RAF base in Singapore from its earliest beginnings, through the golden era of the flying-boats, its capture in WW2 and on to its closure in the 1970s. **£15.00**

The RAF & Me • Former Stirling navigator **Gordon Frost** recalls ops with 570 Sqn from RAF Harwell, including 'Market-Garden' 'Varsity' and others. *'A salute to the mighty Stirling and its valiant crews.'* **£9.95**

Training for Triumph • **Tom Docherty's** very thorough account of the amazing achievement of RAF Training Command, who trained over 90,000 aircrew during World War 2. *'An impressively detailed book.'* **£12.00**

To Strive and Not to Yield An inspiring account of the involvement of No 626 Squadron RAF Bomber Command in the 'Battle of Berlin' (1943/44) and a salute to the men and women who served on the squadron. **£14.95**

Un Grand Bordel • Geoffrey French relates air-gunner **Norman Lee**'s amazing real-life adventures with the French Maquis (Secret Army) after being shot down over Europe. *"Frequently funny and highly eventful."*   £9.95

UXB Vol 2 More unusual and gripping tales of bomb disposal in WW2 and after.   £9.95

Wot! No Engines? • Alan Cooper tells the story of military gliders in general and the RAF glider pilots who served on Operation Varsity in 1945 in particular. A very large and impressive book with many photos.   £18.00

While Others Slept • Former Hampden navigator **Eric Woods** tells the story of Bomber Command's early years and how he completed a tour of duty with 144 Squadron. *'Full of valuable historical detail.'*   £9.95

WOMEN & WORLD WAR TWO

A WAAF at War • Former MT driver **Diana Lindo**'s charming evocation of life in the WAAF will bring back happy memories to all those who also served in World War 2. *"Nostalgic and good-natured."*   £9.95

Corduroy Days • Warm-hearted and amusing recollections of **Josephine Duggan-Rees**'s wartime years spent as a Land Girl on farms in the New Forest area. *"Funny, nostalgic and very well written."*   £9.95

Ernie • **Celia Savage**'s quest to discover the truth about the death of her father, an RAF Halifax navigator with 149 Sqn, who died in WW2 when she was just 6 years old. *"A real-life detective story."*   £9.95

In My Father's Footsteps • **Pat Bienkowski**'s moving account of her trip to Singapore & Thailand to visit the places where her father and uncle were both POW's during WW2.   £9.95

Lambs in Blue • **Rebecca Barnett's** revealing account of the wartime lives and loves of a group of WAAFs posted to the tropical paradise of Ceylon. *"A highly congenial WW2 chronicle."*   £9.95

Radar Days • Delightful evocation of life in the wartime WAAF by former Radar Operator **Gwen Arnold**, who served at Bawdsey Manor RDF Station, Suffolk. *"Amusing, charming and affectionate."*   £9.95

Searching in the Dark The amusing wartime diary of **Peggy Butler** a WAAF radar operator 1942-1946 – written when she was just 19 yrs old and serving at Bawdsey RDF station in Suffolk   £9.95

MEMOIRS & HISTORIES – NON-MILITARY

20th CenturyFarmers Boy • Sussex farmer **Nick Adames** looks back on a century of rural change and what it has meant to his own family and the county they have farmed in for 400 years.   £9.95

Call an Ambulance! • former ambulance driver **Alan Crosskill** recalls a number of light-hearted episodes from his eventful career in the 1960s/70s. *'Very amusing and entertaining'.*   £9.95

Harry – An Evacuee's Story • The misadventures of **Harry Collins** – a young lad evacuated from his home in Stockport UK to Manitoba, Canada in WW2. *'An educational description of the life of an evacuee'*   £9.95

Just Visiting... • Charming and funny book by former Health Visitor **Molly Corbally**, who brilliantly depicts colourful characters and entertaining incidents from her long career.   £9.95

Occupation Nurse • **Peter & Mary Birchenall** pay tribute to the achievement of the group of untrained nurses who provided healthcare at Guernsey's only hospital during the German occupation of 1940-45.   £9.95

FICTION

A Trace of Calcium by **David Barnett** – A commuter comes to the aid of a young woman in trouble, becomes implicated in murder and must use all his resources to clear his name.   £9.95

Double Time by **David Barnett** – A light-hearted time-travel fantasy in which a bookmaker tries to use a time machine to make his fortune and improve his love-life with hilarious consequences.   £9.95

Last Sunset by **AA Painter** A nautical thriller set in the world of international yachting. A middle aged yachtsman becomes accidentally embroiled with smugglers, pirates and a very sexy young lady...   £9.95

The Brats by **Tony Paul** Tony Paul tells the true story of his grandfather, who, as a boy, along with several friends, stowed away on a ship bound for Canada. The youngsters' brutal mistreatment at the hands of the Captain and Mate of the ship caused a scandal that made headlines in Victorian times. *An enthralling real-life seafaring story.*   £9.95

The Cherkassy Incident by **Hunter Carlyle** A gripping action thriller featuring a terrorist plot to steal nuclear missiles from a sunken Russian nuclear submarine and the efforts of international security agents to stop them.   £9.95

MISCELLANEOUS SUBJECTS

Just a Butcher's Boy by **Christopher Bolton** Charming account of small town life in the 1950s in the rural Leiston, Suffolk and idyllic summers spent with grandparents who owned the local butcher's shop.　　**£5.95**

Impress of Eternity by **Paul McNamee** An investigation into the authenticity of the Turin Shroud. A former schoolmaster examines the evidence and comes to a startling conclusion.　　**£5.95**

Making a Successful Best Man's Speech An indispensable aid to anyone who feels nervous about making a wedding speech. Tells you what to say and how to remember it.　　**£5.95**

Near & Yet So Far by **Audrey Truswell** The founder of an animal rescue charity tells charming and heart-warming tales of the rescue and rehabilitation of many four-legged friends in need.　　**£9.95**

Reputedly Haunted Inns of the Chilterns & Thames Valley by **Roger Long** – A light hearted look at pubs & the paranormal in the Heart of England　　**£5.95**

BOOKS FEATURING THE SOUTH COAST & THE SOUTH DOWNS REGION

A Portrait of Slindon by **Josephine Duggan Rees** A charming history of this attractive and well-preserved West Sussex village, from its earliest beginnings to the present day, taking in the exploits of its many notable residents over the years. Very informative and entertaining. Illustrated with many photos, some in colour.　　**£14.95**

Retribution by **Mike Jupp** An outrageous and very funny comedy/fantasy novel for adults and older children, featuring bizarre goings-on in a quiet English seaside town that bears a striking resemblance to Mike's home town of Bognor Regis. Brilliantly illustrated.　　**£9.95**

Unknown to History and Fame by **Brenda Dixon** – Charming portrait of Victorian life in the West Sussex village of Walberton via the writings of Charles Ayling, a resident of the village, whose reports on local events were a popular feature in *The West Sussex Gazette* over many years during the Victorian era.　　**£9.95**

A Little School on the Downs The story of Harriet Finlay-Johnson, headmistress of a little school junior in Sompting, West Sussex in the 1890s, whose ideas and classroom techniques began a revolution in education. She also scandalised society at the time by marrying a former pupil, 20 years her junior. *An amazing and inspiring true story.*　　**£9.95**

The South Coast Beat Scene of the 1960s The South Coast may not have been as famous as Liverpool in the swinging sixties but it was nevertheless a hotbed of musical activity. Broadcaster **Mike Read** traces the complete history of the musicians, the fans and the venues from Brighton to Bognor in this large and lavishly illustrated book.　　**£24.95**

Boys & Other Animals by **Josephine Duggan Rees**. A charming and delightfully funny account of a mother's many trials and tribulations bringing up a boisterous all-male family on a farm in rural Sussex during the 1950s-70s.　　**£9.95**